REFLECTION OF ONLY YOU

A Guidebook for the Adult Only-Child

JOYMARIE BRANSON

Information about legal documents or transactions mentioned in this book pertains only to the United States. This information is given only as a suggestion, not legal advice.

•••

Reflection of Only You
A Guidebook for the Adult Only-child
JoyMarie Branson

ISBN 978-1-64184-638-7 (Paperback)
ISBN 978-1-64184-639-4 (Ebook)

For the latest news, book details, and other information, visit JoyMarie Branson's official website at
www.joymariellc.com

For information about connecting with other only-children, visit the O² Website at
www.onlysquared.com

Dedication

To all the only-onlys

and

To Mom and Dad

• • •

CONTENTS

INTRODUCTION

A GUIDEBOOK FOR THE ONLY-ONLY (O^2)

This book is for the adult only-child. More specifically, it's for the over fifty-year-old adult only-child, with no children, no significant other, and no extended family. These words are for the adult only-child sitting entirely alone after a parent's death, who hears a deafening silence. This person thinks no one comprehends how alone they feel after both their parents have died. It would help if you had the support and guidance from someone who could grasp being an only-child and can validate someone like you.

A search on the internet for information to help the adult only-child figure out what to do during or after this life-changing event doesn't offer much useful information. You may find a few articles written about only-children. These articles and their comments most often degenerate into competitions between those with and without siblings. If you have children, you may find emotional support available through those relationships. My purpose for this book, though, is to help guide you through the most challenging time in your life and let you know you're not the only-only (O^2).

Because before this, I had no clue at all.

CHAPTER 1
CRISIS MODE

Nine days ago, my mom went into the hospital. I know that I must get her last will and testament completed and signed. Today. I don't think, at least not consciously, that anything is going to happen to her. But I hear a loud voice in my head. I even feel it in my body, telling me to get it done. Today.

Okay, next question, "Who do I know that's a notary or knows of a notary?" A notary is an appointed state government official who serves as an impartial witness when someone signs a vital document. A notary must witness your parent(s) signing their last will and testament. If your parent is in the hospital, you'll need to find a notary who will come there.

Ask your friends or the aides and nurses at the hospital if they can recommend one. Look online or in a business directory. Banks have notaries, which in most cases, is perfect. But those notaries don't come to hospitals. You'll also need two other witnesses not related to you or your parent(s) at the signing. Please note that nurses, aides, or doctors can't witness any legal documents concerning your parent(s) last wishes and assets.

After several texts and phone messages, I scheduled a notary to come to the hospital that afternoon. A half-hour later, I received a text message from the notary. Now she isn't sure if she can do it because my mom is in the hospital. She needs more information about the state of my mom's health and her mental ability. From a legal standpoint, this is of vital importance. She informs me she'll get back to me.

I couldn't give up. If needed, I would find another notary. Something keeps pushing me, telling me it's essential to complete this. Today. Pay attention to the strong feelings you get during an event like this. At 4:00 p.m., the notary sends me a text message confirming that she is coming to the hospital and that the witnesses will be there at 5:00 p.m. There was an urgency, but it was a calm urgency. Are you the one during a crisis who's the calm one? As an only-child, you probably learned this survival skill at an early age. It can suit you well and get you through tough times like these.

I got to the hospital around 3:00 p.m. Two men from my mom's church were there praying with her. A radiology technician was also there, setting up a machine to get a chest X-ray. My mom told me she wasn't feeling well. Besides leukemia, which was rapidly depleting her red and white blood cells, doctors were now monitoring a new malady, pneumonia. My urgency to get the will signed and notarized now, not later, was still there. Over and over that day, I kept hearing, "Don't wait. This is important. Get it done today, not two days from now when you plan to come back."

When they admitted my mom to the hospital, she had a urinary tract infection. She was there for 12 days. During those 12 days, they discovered gout in her foot and elbow, confirmed she had an aggressive form of leukemia through a bone marrow biopsy, and now she had pneumonia. The infection and gout had compromised her immune system, making it even harder for her body to fight the leukemia, and the pneumonia complicated everything. And then she died.

Not That Long Ago

It had been only two years since my dad's back surgery, his cancer diagnosis, and his three-month stay in the hospital and a rehabilitation facility. He was 83 years old, and the cancer had compromised his body, so there was no need to cause more damage by treating it with radiation or chemotherapy. Several times it appeared it would conquer him, but he would rally, only to go downhill a little further the next time. I figured God still had plans for him, or me, or someone else.

There's not always an answer for why it works out the way it does. It's not clear why a parent continues to hang on to life. Death affects more than just your small circle. Perhaps your parent will say or do something that affects someone's life during the time in which they seem to hang on to life by a thread. Or perhaps you'll notice the people who don't have an emotional attachment to the person who's dying or has died are the most sympathetic and helpful during those times.

If your parent(s) died recently, most likely you're numb and don't feel connected to anything. Or you may feel attached to everything. There will be intermittent flip-flopping back and forth from one extreme to the other. Most people will have no clue anything is even wrong with you. Only-children are experts at hiding their genuine feelings if needed. It's hard to share this profound hurt. It may be the first time in your life you've experienced deep feelings like these. For me, this was true.

I realized I had these deep feelings only for these two people, my parents. I thought I loved my other relatives, but this love for my parents made it seem I had just liked my other relatives. The extreme pain of losing my parents was like losing an appendage. An invisible part of me was missing in a sudden and profound way.

There was no plan in place when my dad died. There had been three months to talk about it, but we hadn't. People don't like to talk about death. As an only-child, I had always thought about when these times would come. I had tried to distance myself and my feelings from the upcoming event, so it or they wouldn't overwhelm me when I needed to be fully present.

Confirm that there are instructions for what to do after your parent dies. I found out my thoughts were just that, just notions, not facts. I had the idea he'd written step-by-step instructions for me, and I would pull out a piece of paper and follow it like a textbook. How I wish I had asked, because that wasn't the case. There were no instructions. There was only my incomplete knowledge of the process, which wasn't useful as a guidebook.

Being unattached to your emotions will serve you. It'll help you do the tasks you need to do. It doesn't mean you don't care. It means you realize those feelings won't help you at that moment. But never think you don't care — no matter what may have happened in your relationship with your parents — you care. But it's okay not to feel anything right now.

CHAPTER 2
WHAT YOU THINK YOU KNOW

I didn't know how to have those conversations with my parents. Or how important it was to have them before they were in the hospital. When they were in the hospital, I was so stressed out just trying to navigate and figure everything out; there wasn't time, and I couldn't think about it. I only had a few hours with my mom. It didn't seem possible that she would die soon, even though the doctors said the tests confirmed there was no positive outcome. My dad had held on for a few months after his terminal diagnosis, and I guess I thought she would, too. I presumed she was just as tough as he was, even more so.

Now that they're both gone, I know so much more than I did when they were alive. I'm not sure my parents or I ever realized how important they were to my life. They were an enormous part. Despite all the hurtful and sometimes horrendous things that transpired throughout my life, they had been my pillars. They were always there. Even when I had limited or no contact with them, I was aware of their presence. They were still there. If I needed help, one of them would be there for me. This was ironic because I always thought I had been self-sufficient.

Many times throughout my life, I had wished them gone. All I wanted was to stop this feeling of letting them down. I had taken on the shame, guilt, and blame in our dysfunctional little family and thought I must be the reason they were unhappy and angry all the time. My conclusion was that I was an awful daughter. To them, it appeared, I made these big decisions and significant changes in my life without a care or a thought about the world around me. I was sure they didn't think I ever listened to anything they said. I always figured if things didn't work out, well, I would pick myself up, dust off my butt, and go on to the next thing. That was something they never realized I had learned from them both.

Who's Taking Care of Whom?

I suck at taking care of people. I've never cared for anyone except myself, some boyfriends I have lived with, and my ex-husband. Although ironic, yes, even though my parents hadn't been there for me growing up, which they weren't, I thought it was my responsibility to take on the colossal duty of their care at the end. It was a task at which I thought I would be inadequate. During my dad's last months, I am thankful I had my mom's daily support on the phone. She understood how he was and how difficult it was for me to attend to him. Other relatives on my dad's side of the family didn't know him the way we did.

After my mom died, I didn't have daily support from someone who had known her the way I did. Yes, my best friend was aware of some history, but I didn't want to be a burden when she already had her own health and family issues. Had she been a sister, I would've added to her commitments without a second thought. I still wouldn't have enjoyed doing that, but because she would have been a sibling and shared an emotional connection to the person who died, I would've concluded she should share those responsibilities.

I didn't think I would find myself parent-less, sibling-less, child-less, and significant-other-less at 55 years old. Wasn't I too young for all this to happen? I guess I hadn't thought past the fear of when it would happen or how it would happen. What would my parents expect of me, and would I be able to meet those expectations? Losing them both within two years of each other was overwhelming.

Of course, I had thought about it happening. But I hadn't thought about what happened after my parent(s) died. Other things started going through my head, too. I hadn't even thought about how living across the street from my father for 15 years had affected me, how it had given me a false sense of safety. Although, in my defense, I was too afraid of him to think of how he was dispelling my hidden fears.

I got my strength from them, and I got my tenacity from them. And a lot of anger, too. How is it that, as an adult, I felt safe with the two people who neglected to keep me safe as a child? Then I remember they weren't aware of the earlier abuse that had happened to me. Would things have been different if they had known? People call what I was feeling unconditional love, and it was happening among the three of us the whole time. They may have been aware of it because they were parents. I wasn't aware of it, as I wasn't a parent, I didn't think I had that kind of love for anyone.

I never realized how much of what I did throughout my life was because of my parents. On a subconscious level, I was always trying to get their attention or praise. But now, there is a lot more freedom to be myself. I realize I don't have to please anyone anymore. There is no absolute or perfect way to do things to get my parents or anyone else's approval. Now I'm the only one concerned about whether I do it the right way or the wrong way, or if it qualifies as a wonderful or a terrible thing. I wish I could've figured that out earlier.

Being a Version of Me for Them

Discussions with my parents about my future didn't include me, ever. I found notes my mom wrote mentioning conversations they had about a few of those decisions. Decisions I made, or thought I made, on my own. The reality was they had manipulated me into doing what they thought was in my best interest. The one she wrote about in the notes happened when I was 26 years old. For the previous 10 years, I had been financially independent, even though I went through a few bumpy years. My parents had a conference about my future. Without me, of course. My mom believed that I was in an abusive relationship, and they decided that I should move from the west coast to the east coast where my dad lived. They also thought it was a good idea for my grandmother to accompany me. You know, to make sure that I made it there. I had talked to them both about the move, but separately. It was a mistake to think they hadn't spoken to each other after their divorce when I was fourteen.

For all I know, this manipulation happened behind the scenes throughout my entire life. It explained why their absence was so profound. Did you find any notes left behind? Clues to a past event, you had always wondered what "that" was all about? Were your parents pulling strings behind the scenes in your life too?

I didn't think my mom thought I was pretty, or at least that's the story I had told myself. My weight became a problem starting when I was around eight years old. When I was nine years old, my mom put me on my first diet. I got braces when I was ten years old and had to wear the pre-requisite headgear contraption to fix my overbite. It made me feel like an alien! When I began ninth grade, the braces came off right before I turned fourteen. The weight, the braces, the headgear, the teenage acne, and my growing shyness would've been enough, but coupled with wanting to please her more than anything, I was on a course destined to fail.

In contrast, I didn't think my dad cared about my physical attributes. It seemed the only thing I ever did that impressed him, was when I gave up my life and showed up to take care of him. In fact, he even told me that. It hurt then and still stings now because I didn't know how he thought I had ever "not" loved him. I didn't like him much, but love wasn't negotiable, no matter what he did. The same was valid for the feelings I had about my mom.

I also thought he didn't care about my mental attributes, either. It didn't impress him when I got all A's in my Digital Media classes for my associate's degree. Classes where I had to be technically savvy and creative. His comment was I could've done it years ago. What I heard was that I hadn't lived my life according to his timeline for my life. I was 42 years old when I got my degree. While taking those classes, I taught part-time at the same college in the evening, worked a full-time job during the day as a web developer, and was going through a tough time in my marriage. But none of that had impressed him.

Unknown to me, there had been money for me to go to college when I was younger, but it was contingent on my grad-uating from high school. I didn't graduate from high school, but I got my GED the same year I would've graduated. I guess my parents, neither of whom had completed high school, didn't know colleges and universities accepted a GED just like a diploma. Much later, I found out it was another one of those discussions where my parents conferenced about my life without including me.

For a long time, I thought the reason people had children was so there was someone to do all the housework. Because I was the only-child, I had to do "all" the chores. I never received an allowance for those chores, but my friends did. I never understood why I didn't, but I never asked my parents why, either. When I was around ten years old, I stated I didn't want to have children. When I was in my mid-forties and told this to my therapist, she remarked it was because I didn't have an available role model for what a parent should be. She was right.

There was a lot of emotional pain when I was growing up. There were a lot of things I didn't discern. I never wanted a child to have those feelings. I thought I would destroy any relationship I might have with "my children" because I would be so overprotective of them. I joked that I would duct-tape them to the refrigerator to keep them safe from all the deranged predators in the world. But the voice in my head didn't think I was joking!

Holidays made me anxious. I still don't know why my mom never let me help her decorate the Christmas tree. Was she afraid I would get hurt? Was it because I wouldn't do it the way she wanted? I could provide a few more reasons, but it still leaves me at a loss. It could explain why every year, starting when I was around six or seven years old, I started getting sick around Christmas.

One year, instead of the traditional candy-filled Easter basket, they gave me a molded-sugar egg. The hollowed-out halves came together with a pretty decorative sugar border. A scene made from colored sugar filled the hollowed-out area. I don't remember what the scene was, but I remember it was charming, and then the other thing I remember is it tasted really, really good. My mom was furious and appalled when she found out I had eaten it. I was eleven; it was Easter; it was the only thing I had received. No one told me not to eat it! It was just another time they forgot I wasn't an adult. After that, I never cared much for Easter.

Being a Version of Me for Them, Too

In most relationships, I try to be everything for that person, which only leaves me feeling angry and stressed out. Those expectations are self-imposed. No one puts those expectations on me. I thought it was more important for me to love you than for you to love me. Every time anyone has even asked me what I needed, I shrugged and answered I didn't know. Because I didn't. I needed the basics: food, water, and a roof over my head; anything more was extra, and I could take care of those, too. I always hoped they would help me figure out what I needed. "What? You have needs? You didn't mention it in the last ten years we've been together!"

I'm also not adept at managing my anger. It hides underneath the surface, and then when it gets too much, it boils over and sometimes explodes. I've always disliked arguments, and then I married a man who wouldn't argue with me, which was even more frustrating! One time I had a bag of takeout food, and I got so angry when he wouldn't argue back with me that I threw my bag of food at him. He responded by raising his eyebrows and eyeing me like I was crazy. Anger is never an enjoyable dish for any relationship.

When I was growing up, my mom packed up and left many times. All I remember was when I came home from school, I would find out she had left, and my dad would be angry. As a child, I didn't realize his anger was a cover for his actual feelings. No one ever explained to me why she left or why she came back. The child in me assumed it was my fault, and I was sure I had done something that made her go. Another aspect of me knew I hadn't, but a child can't rationalize those types of adult situations. As an only-child, I didn't have a sibling to help me figure it out, either. I thought you would leave me if I wasn't good enough or disappointed you in my later adult relationships.

The Only-child Stereotype

It still surprises me whenever I tell someone I'm an only-child, and they reply with a trite stereotypical response. For years people have believed these stereotypes because of published psychology papers and the opinions of those who know nothing about being an only-child. Public policies and society educate us to be tolerant of everyone and their differences. But people still stereotype only-children, even adult only-children. Those labels imply something is wrong with us. As young children, it can degrade our spirits, and we protect ourselves from them. We hadn't chosen to be an only-child.

It doesn't go over well when you make comments to someone because of their skin color, sexual identity, or place in the family hierarchy. In fact, they can sue you for defamation of character or violating their rights. When I ask people who have siblings, "How would you feel if people said degrading things about you just because you have siblings?" their response is they wouldn't like it. Who would?

Many only-children struggle with self-esteem issues related to these comments. The misconceptions about who they are as a "person" causes them to think they must change who they are. Why are we labeled spoiled, entitled, or selfish? Why are we labeled at all? Should we feel ashamed for having the love and attention of our parents? Or, in my case, and for many other only-children, not having the love and attention from them? It's difficult to not take these rude remarks to heart.

As a collective group, we're a minority. As a minority, we suffered degrading remarks when we were children made by our peers and adults, leaving us to wonder, *Did we do something wrong? Is there something wrong with me?* If we decried the challenges of being an only-child, they told us, "Everyone has it rough." Examine those last sentences, think about these words—minority, suffered as children at the hand of adults, quieted about our challenges when we were children and later as adults. How do you feel about those words?

Not all only-children are lonely, scared, or healing from enmeshed relationships with their parents. Many do well for the same reasons people with siblings do well. They had the love and nurturing from parents or extended family members when they were growing up. But regardless of whether you received that care, when the time comes to care for sick parents and deal with everything after they die on your own, these things will affect you too.

When I had to cease my parent's medical treatments because it was more humane to just make them as comfortable as possible, the loneliness was overwhelming. My father pressed on for longer than I thought he would, and it was a relief for both of us when he died. When I left the rehabilitation facility the night before he died, I told him it was okay for him to go, and I would be "okay." I lied for his benefit. Three days before my mom died, she asked me if I was going to be okay. I lied and said, "Yes." Now that they're both gone, I can say there are many days I'm not okay.

REFLECTION OF ONLY YOU   15

My Type

I used to tell people my dad was a "do it my way, or don't do it at all" type, and my mom was a "do it right or don't do it at all" type. This meant I was a "do it my way, do it right, or don't do it at all" type. They would chuckle, not knowing how serious I was. Trying to please my parents my entire life honed my perfectionism. I didn't realize the magnitude of that until after they both had died. It also carried over into my professional life. The moment I put someone in an authority position over me, I thought I needed to be flawless for them. No wonder I'm so exhausted.

It could also explain why at two separate times, when I got to the top of the proverbial ladder, I tossed it aside. When most people arrive at the top, they don't leave. But not me. As soon as I reached that peak, I would get bored and consider the next thing I could grow up to be. Something even better, something that would make my parents, and anyone else I was trying to please, proud of me. Sometimes that person was me. I'm not saying I didn't feel proud of my accomplishments. I did. But I was also demanding of myself. I was 54 years old the first time I remember my mom saying she was proud of me. She may have thought it, but that was the only time I ever remember hearing it.

I didn't think I would feel lost like this, not knowing what to do and questioning life. What's it all about? Who's it all for? Who am I leaving it to? No one will see any importance in any of my photos. No one will feel anything except burdened to have to go through all my "stuff" when I die. I must remind myself it won't worry me at all because I'll be dead. I won't even care. Not one bit. My problem with that realization is, "Then what am I supposed to care about?"

Some assert relationships with others are the most important. Or making a positive impact on the environment, or pursuing a noble cause, is what it's all about. Those are the things you spend your life "doing." Some parents convince themselves that giving children to the world is their most important contribution in life. Making sure the family name continues, heritage, family values, blah, blah, blah. I'm sure several of them will do amazing things and help others, but they didn't do those things because they were trying to determine what their purpose was in life. They're a mom, a dad, a brother, a sister, an aunt, an uncle, a grandparent, etc. That's part of their fulfillment in life.

I'm thankful I'm comfortable being alone; I think I'd have an even harder time if it wasn't the case. For me, being alone can be a comfort I can't find around others. The only one I must worry about pleasing is myself, and that's a lot harder than it sounds. I must remember to be kind to myself and let myself off the hook when I don't adjust well or do everything correctly the first time.

CHAPTER 3
HELLO, I'M GLAD YOU'RE HERE

I'm happy we've found each other in this space. You're not alone; you'll be okay, and we can get through this together. We can talk about a lot while you're here within these pages. My goal is to supply you with a template of sorts, a guidebook to give you a place to start. A place that will provide comfort for you, to let you know you belong and you fit in. We all have our stories. A few of them are great, and a few of them are not. Regardless, those stories are our stories. More importantly, we're all only-children, which gives us the gifts, abilities, and talents to fulfill a unique purpose.

A Place to Start

Don't give up now. This is where you can start. Where you can heal. First, acquaint yourself with the unique qualities you have because you're an only-child. So be okay with the uniqueness and let go of any shame placed upon you. You don't need to feel any guilt about being an only-child. If someone should mistake your originality as a flaw, remind them even the most brilliant diamonds are flawed, but they reflect the light just the same. That's what it's about. It's about the light of who you are shining within you, how it reflects, how you cover it up, or how at other times, you let it shine.

If you've suffered a recent loss, first, thank you for being here, and second, it's okay if you don't feel anything right now – except as you read this book, you'll start to feel better, perhaps find a purpose for your life. You know how to get through this. Deep down, you know it won't all be perfect, and even though it will feel uncomfortable, I've learned sometimes it's okay to feel uncomfortable. It's when the best things can happen. I'm sorry for your loss or losses and the pain you feel or the lack thereof. It doesn't help to say it'll pass or get better because you don't feel or even think like that now, and that's okay. You're here, and together we can get through these challenges.

It's difficult to explain to someone how it feels to lose a parent, and even more so, to explain how the only-child feels. Someone with siblings has different thoughts about it. You may just now realize that you're alone – really alone. It's a terrifying place. You may have never understood how connected you were to your parent(s), and you may have experienced a massive, catastrophic wound when they died. This is normal. In case no one has told you, you'll find a unique perspective about what has happened and perceive the "whys" in time.

How You See Things

In time, you'll see things in a way you never allowed yourself to see before. You may feel love, anger, jealousy, gratefulness, or kindness toward your parent(s) in a way you never thought possible. You're here to be healed, to receive guidance that will help you through this time. Where do we start? My objective for you is that you can have those conversations with your parent(s) before you find yourself in the position to be more responsible than you've ever had to be. Death isn't something we want to talk about, and we each have our reasons.

Do you have a view about death? How comfortable do you think you are talking about it to others? If your loss is recent, and you're struggling to find your way through this space, let's walk through it together. First, relax and take a deep breath. Let me guide you and help you with this enormous task. Let me be a resource and a guide, a friend, one of your people. And that's an important question. Do you know who your people are? Are you getting the support you need? Do you feel the people who support you are "supporting" you? Can you remove yourself from those who aren't helpful? Are you able to ask them for the space or the help you need?

Are you used to asking for help? Only-children are by nature, independent, especially when you've had to rely on yourself a lot throughout your life. More than once, you've found you had the ability, and you have gotten through (where did that strength come from?) more than you thought possible. Sometimes there just wasn't anyone, and that's okay, too. That's when you listen to the voice inside you, the one you feel the most comfortable listening to. Remember, this is where your strength lies, the power of one. But right now, you may need to ask for help, which I know may not be easy to do.

When I experienced my mom's death, I needed a lot of help, but most people don't know how to deal with grief and loss in helpful ways; at least, that was my experience. It seemed like the most useful people had no emotional connection to the person who died. For instance, the people at the hospital or the funeral director and the people at the funeral home may seem to be the only sane people around you. Try to find more people like them. They'll help you keep your sanity. Take another deep breath, reach out to someone, reach out to me if you have no one. It's why I'm here.

On those days right before and after each of my parents died was when I felt the most alone. I had always known this time would come. But no one had prepared me for how alone I would feel when these two people, the most important people in my life, weren't there and were never coming back. The realization hit me that there was nothing I could ever do to change it. It was just me. They hadn't prepared me to understand these things.

The safety support wires, the ones I hadn't even been aware of, and which held me so tight, had disappeared. That safety net had disappeared. Restrictions and their expectations disappeared, too. I had limited myself for so long, just trying to get an appropriate reaction from them. This loss, though, had taught me it doesn't matter what the relationship was before they died. After they have died, you'll see it in ways that were never visible to you.

I want your regrets to be few, and if you still have your parent(s), I anticipate that this guidebook will lessen those regrets. It'll help you focus on the essential things. You can have those crucial conversations with them or not, and make those choices before you're dealing with an irreversible loss.

DNRs, Wills, Estates, and Trusts

It's time to ask some tough questions now. If one or both of your parents are still alive, I hope you can work side-by-side to avoid the grief of unanswered questions. If they've already died, your grief may feel so heavy you may feel it will crush you. It could do that, but it's your choice, although I don't think you need me to tell you that.

If your parent is in the hospital, you must address hospital-specific paperwork right away. A doctor or nurse will ask you about these papers if your parent can't fill them out themselves. These papers include a Do Not Resuscitate (DNR) order. This is a legal order stating not to provide life-saving protocols should your parent's heart stop beating or they stop breathing. If no known DNR exists at the time of the emergency, first responders or health-care personnel must provide life-saving measures as needed to keep your parent alive.

My dad didn't have a DNR on file the day he stopped breathing on an elevator ride from the ICU to his hospital room. They intubated him, and he was unconscious and on a breathing machine for three days. I received a phone call telling me this news when I was more than 3,000 miles away, packing up my belongings. Unfortunately, there was no other family nearby or at the hospital with him. By the time I arrived a few weeks later, he'd regained consciousness, and the hospital released him to a rehabilitation facility. Now there was time to ask him about his wishes and help him fill out the DNR papers, but I still needed signatures from witnesses.

I approached a family in the waiting room at the rehabilitation facility. I didn't know them, and they didn't know me, but there were no family or friends nearby to ask. The family at the rehabilitation facility who were available to help were perfect and right on time. They didn't feel uneasy or inconvenienced by my approach. In fact, they were glad to help. My mom's DNR was on file with her doctor before her hospitalization. That's the best-case scenario.

If your parent goes to a rehabilitation facility, the facility will want to know where they will go when released from their care. Will they be returning home, go to a nursing home, or assisted-living facility? My father could not return to his home for many reasons, and I didn't feel I could give him the level of care he needed. You also must figure out how to pay for those services. Check with your parent's insurance to find out which services they cover. Only in rare cases will health insurance cover the cost of assisted-living or nursing-home facilities.

My dad had served in the military in the 1950s, and he was eligible to go to a Veterans Nursing Home in the state where he lived. If you have this benefit, keep in mind those facilities can have long waiting lists. Contact them as soon as you think you need to move someone into this facility. Your parent's doctor will fill out the paperwork from the nursing home. Specific health issues can help move them closer to the top of the admission list. You will need to provide the paperwork verifying your parent's enlistment and discharge from service. Contact the facility in your state for more specific information. There may also be more than one facility located in your state, so make sure to check availability at each one.

Is there a will? If your parent(s) are still alive and they don't have one, stop reading right now and either get a lawyer or go online and order a Do It Yourself (DIY) last will and testament kit. In most states in the U.S., you can download one and fill in the blanks. For the last will and testament, you will need two witnesses. They can be family friends, your friends, or your coworkers. They can also be complete strangers.

Depending on the size of the estate … "Wait, what's an estate? How would I know the size? What is the size based on?" An estate is any possessions your parent(s) own and includes money, property (land, houses, cars, boats, motorcycles, etc.), retirement accounts, life insurance, pensions, bank accounts, anything with a monetary value. What about the priceless things? That would be everything, wouldn't it? The excellent news here is that if you're the sole heir, none of it will matter much because you inherit everything. If the estate is large, a trust might have been established before your parent(s) died.

Okay, you may ask, "What's a trust?" A trust is a legal document completed in addition to a last will and testament. The Internal Revenue Service (IRS) defines it in the simplest terms, as a three-party arrangement in which the founder of the trust (commonly known as the donor, grantor, or settlor, aka your parent) transfers the legal title of the trust property to a trustee (a fiduciary with regard to the property) to hold and to manage for a third party (the trust's beneficiary). After the trustor's death, they'll disperse the possessions to the heirs named in the trust. Setting up a trust can help reduce taxes and negate the need to go through the probate process after someone dies. But if you're like most of us in the middle-to-lower-class, meaning you've got a little, but not a lot, it's less likely a trust is in place.

Get a notebook or an expandable folder and keep your notes in it. It doesn't matter whether you write them on paper or use a virtual method. It's essential to keep records. Get the day, time, the name of the person you spoke to, the phone number or email of the person you contacted, and any other relevant information from the interaction. It's beneficial to have both a physical and a virtual record; this will help you keep track of everything.

Perfect Timing

You're here at a valuable time if you read this before your parent(s) has died. It also means the most important thing to do at this moment is to stop reading this book. Yes, stop right now. Have that conversation with your parent(s) and get a last will and testament in place. This is by far the most crucial step of all. Should something unexpected happen before you can get the next steps done, this will be your saving grace, and you'll thank yourself many times for completing this. It'll only cost you a little minor work and time. The process is much more challenging if you don't have a will and the unexpected happens, and your parent dies. You can't complete a last will and testament after they've died.

If you've followed this advice, you now have a signed, witnessed, and notarized last will and testament. You'll have completed the most critical part of all the tasks. Your parent(s) should also complete paperwork for a Power of Attorney. You can find this paperwork online, and just like the last will and testament, you'll need witnesses and a notary. This paperwork will allow you to complete financial and legal transactions in their place should they become incapacitated. You can only use a Power of Attorney when your parent(s) is living. After they've died, the allowance is no longer valid.

Another essential task is to ask them about the property that they own. Where's it located? Where are the titles or deeds? Are there are any mortgages or loans associated with the property? If your parents have divorced, the properties are probably separate. After my mom died, I found a title to a piece of property in a state other than where she lived. I didn't know my mom owned this property; it was something her mom had willed to her. There may be different rules in other states concerning getting the property transferred to your name. I contacted a lawyer in that state and was told I'd have to go through the probate process there and pay the applicable fees. Those fees cost more than the property is worth.

Also, ask them about any insurance policies and the beneficiaries of those policies. My parents divorced when I was 14, and my father died when I was 53. He had a life-insurance policy that still listed my mom as the beneficiary, and she was the beneficiary of his pension benefit. Your parent(s) may need to change or update those policies.

Trust me, both your parents realize you'll be alone when they die, even if they don't acknowledge it. They may feel stereotypical guilt about it. That's a societal thing. Consider how we're caught up in that! Societal prejudices aren't your friend. They may feel the guilt, they might not want to think of that for you, and there is the possibility those feelings will come up as part of the beneficial discussions you need to have.

Ask them today. In fact, stop reading now and go ask. It's okay if your parent(s) are hesitant. Again, no one likes to talk about this death thing. We all act as if it won't happen, at least not anytime soon, and we can take care of these crucial tasks tomorrow. An unknown such as death creates an odd fear, which isn't always explainable. It's going to be challenging to ask them these questions, but it'll be much tougher on you later if you haven't put these things in place or know all the things you need to know, or, at least, where to find the information you need.

Keep in mind that if the hospital prescribes an opiate pain medication for them, the answers to those legal questions will become your responsibility. Even though they may be cognitive, they're not of sound mind to make their own decisions. These discussions and decisions are so much easier to address if they're not lying in a hospital bed and impossible to address if they unexpectedly die.

CHAPTER 4
LET'S TALK ABOUT THIS DEATH THING

No one wants to talk about it. We don't seem to get around to the discussion. Maybe your parent(s) are excellent at being adults, and they put everything in order and have things spelled out step-by-step for you when they die. If they did, that's wonderful! You are way ahead of most people! Having it all in order and in place for you doesn't happen often. In fact, I've found this is rare.

Why? I believe it's because death isn't something we want to talk about within the context of living, no matter how agreeable the familial bonds. It makes us too aware it will happen, and we don't have control over it. We have this uncanny ability to function as if we're going to live forever, as if death only happens to someone else. If I had children, I would like to talk to them about this, but I have those same fears. How can we get past these fears? How can we convince our parents, before those crucial times, to sit with us as adults, speak to us as an adult, and make this more comfortable for the person left behind?

My mom told me there was a briefcase with the essential papers in it, and where it was. But she didn't show it to me or go over with me in person what was in it. So, upon her unexpected death, I couldn't even remember where she'd told me it was. A few days later, I found it, because I needed to pick up her death certificate, and I would need her birth certificate to get that. I found nothing in the briefcase about her last wishes. Where is the step-by-step guide for me to follow so I know what to do next?

Both my parents had siblings or significant others to help them when their parents died. My father's parents died many years before I was born. My mom was in her thirties when her father died and, in her sixties when her mother died. I've wondered if it crossed their mind, "Hey, we should sit down and go over this critical life-changing event with our daughter. How can we make it easier for her?"

Go Ask Them

If you haven't talked to your parent(s) about what they want for their funeral or memorial service, go ask them. Don't wait! Stop, put this book down! Go ask them! Yes, it's that important. You may find they're open to talking to you about it, or they may not be. Don't let that stop you. Don't let it get in the way. If you don't ask, you won't know. Why not change that now, while you can? What's stopping you?

It's important to talk to them about their wishes, but it is also essential to speak with them about having the finances to provide for those wishes. If you can put a plan in place now, it'll be more likely to be the reality when the time comes. If not, you may have to figure it out as you go. Honor your ideals and morals. Remember, you're the only one who has to be okay with what you do after they die, regardless of any plan. After they die, there are some decisions you can't change, such as choosing the burial of the body versus cremation of the body. Do what you feel is right if you don't have a plan or know their wishes.

Other people, who may or may not be family members, likely will give you their opinion during these times. My best advice is to listen and take notes. Just remember you're the only one who has to be okay with your decisions. These people will not be around afterward, and if they are, the decisions won't affect them the way they'll affect you.

If your parent has died, you'll have lots and lots of questions you don't have answers for. Find someone to chat with if you're finding it too complicated. Remember, I'm here, and the only-only (O^2) community is also there for you.

Is There a Plan?

Plan if you can; that's the most beneficial scenario. My best advice would be to do what you would do for yourself if you find yourself here and don't know what to do. What would you want someone to do for you if they were in your shoes right now? Finances will be an enormous factor in these decisions, as well as your beliefs about spending those finances. If you can plan and pay ahead of time, then you've nothing more to do. It may be possible to change it later, depending on the plan. Talk with your parent(s) about changing it if you need to when the time comes. You may find yourself in a different financial situation after they die.

I never understood why you would spend so much money to bury someone. I never wanted to view someone lying in a casket. To me, the body was an empty shell, a grotesque version of them. The makeup didn't help, either. They never, ever appeared like that in actual life. It wasn't helpful to me, but I guess it is for others. Be careful to not take on someone else's comfort level. Your comfort level may not be the same. And it's okay. It doesn't make you wrong if you're not like other people. You need not do what's comfortable for them. You need to honor your own feelings and what is best for you.

It's okay to have your own ideas and feelings about all of this. Others should respect them, even if they're different. If there are no instructions, no plan prepared and paid for ahead of time, do what you would do for yourself and don't spend a ton of money. It'll impress no one, and not spending a ton of money will embarrass no one, either. If you believe your parent(s) can see what you're doing after they die, remember they only gaze at you with love now. Just love.

If you're reading this before your parent(s) have died, stop and go call them, or go speak to them. Now! Ask them about their last wishes and let them know that it's essential for you to understand what they want and plan it together if possible. That may or may not be possible. If it gets too hard, you may need another person, a mediator who can help with the plans.

I thought there was a plan for my dad, and when I realized there wasn't, then I did what I thought was best for me. My dad was gone. The decisions I made would not affect him. There wasn't much money; I no longer had an income because I abandoned my business and life to move and come care for him, and at the moment, I had no idea where or how my future would turn out. It didn't seem like a beneficial idea to spend a lot of money on a funeral where three people would show up. Any family who showed up would do so out of obligation to him, and that wasn't something I wanted them to feel they had to do. It was no longer essential to him. If it had been, he'd have left those instructions, and it wasn't necessary to me.

The First Phone Calls to Make

The first phone call will be to a funeral home after the hospital calls to tell you your parent has died, or the coroner confirms their death if they died at home. If your parent has donated their body to an organization, call the organization. The funeral home or donation organization will plan to pick up the body and take it to their facility.

This will happen quickly. Frankly, when I think back, I remember little about those conversations or how most of the process ensued. I was on autopilot. If the body is going to a funeral home, they will need to know if you plan a burial or cremation. You may also need to make this decision within a short amount of time. If you're distressed, tell the funeral home this is the first time you've dealt with someone's death.

Let them know you're an only-child, and you don't have any family to help you. Ask the questions, even the ones you think are stupid. Keep in mind the stupid ones are the most important! Don't feel ashamed if you don't have the funds. Don't be shy about asking them if there is any funding available to help you. If your parent was in the Armed Forces or served as a public servant (for example, my dad was a firefighter), there may be help available to pay for some expenses. It may be hard if you're sitting there alone like I was. Ask anyway.

I struggled with feeling shame around my thoughts about how crazy it was to spend tons of money on an empty body. I thought there were other ways, better ways, you could remember someone. To my surprise, there was a way to lower the cost by more than a third. If I hadn't asked, I wouldn't have known this was possible. Like many others, you might pay those fees and expenses and find out later there were funds available to reduce the costs. For my dad, a $4,000 funeral became a $1,000 simple cremation. Was it a fancy, over-the-top showy thing? No, not at all.

The people who work at the funeral home will be the most empathetic toward you during this time and may appear to be more caring than your family or friends. Your family and friends may not know the answers to the questions you have, and the people who work at the funeral home have no emotions attached to the person who died. That's the way it should be.

I'm not saying their sympathy and compassion are fake. In professions that deal with death, the practitioners must have boundaries. They need to limit how much they care about you personally and how much care they give to you. You can't feel the emotions of those around you at a deep level continuously and still do your job well. This is how it should be, and it's how you want it to be.

It Doesn't Have to Be Done Right Now

You need to stop again, put this book down, and ask yourself if you need a break or if it is better to continue. Stay in touch with yourself and know whether you can manage this. Realize you might break down, and that's okay. If you need to get mad and throw something or yell, then do that. Try not to yell at others. They're feeling a lot of emotions too, and they may yell back at you!

The most important thing to do is to make sure you're checking in with yourself. You won't want to do this, but try to feel a little of what's going on. You won't want those feelings to be your reality. If you can notice them, though, it'll help you. Do something you like to do, which has nothing to do with these plans. Don't let anyone tell you must do anything right this minute. Yes, a few things have timelines and deadlines, but most of those have grace periods.

You may think you want to get things done as soon as you can. Get those tasks completed and off your list. You know, be the responsible one, and all that. Remember, sometimes being proactive can work against you during this time. I found that most things can wait, or you may have to wait to do them. If you're curious, see the links to the checklists in the back of this book.

It's okay to give yourself a few days. People will share their advice, so take notes, and thank them, but get by yourself to figure out what you should do. You don't have to close accounts or give away things yet. Double-check with the funeral home or donation organization, as they can contact the Social Security Administration on your parent(s) behalf. If your parent received Social Security, that's the only government obligation you must complete within those first few days.

If you don't have support, no worries, you have me; I'm your people. If you need someone to listen, I can do that. I can offer suggestions, but keep in mind, they're just suggestions. I can relate to you on the only-child level, the one saying, "I feel I'm all alone, and no one seems to know how I feel." You're not alone, and I understand how you feel.

CHAPTER 5
AND YOU ARE?

Have you ever heard the remark that goes something like, "When someone with a sizeable estate dies, that's when the relatives come out of the woodworks?" Neither of my parent's estates was worth enough for anyone but a petty thief to care. My worry was whether any "unknown secret relatives" were going to come out of the woodwork. Then my next question was, "Did I want to know them if they did?" How can you protect yourself from that? What if you don't want to know them or the secrets?

Family or Friends

Perhaps when I was younger, I wished for a sibling. My two cousins, a brother and sister who were older than I, lived with us for about a year and a half while their father was overseas in the military. So, when I was five years old, I experienced what it would be like to have instant siblings. I must've not liked it much, because I didn't want them to come back and live with us. They were cousins, not siblings, and I never felt like their sister. They came and then went.

Did you create your own family from your close friends? Or even adopting their family as your family? I had several "moms" in my life and still do, but those relationships are still missing something. It's not the same connection you have with your mom. Even if you don't care for your mom much, it's not the same. What I found interesting was that until after my father died, I had no substitute fathers.

I wondered if the emotional connection with siblings was similar to the relationship with the parents. From what I've read, the answer is yes; it's still the same deep connection. These people know more about you and who you are because you saw them every day and spent so much time with them. These were the formative years, the years we contemplate and assert had such an impact on us and who we are. They're the years and the experiences we'll use later to blame others for who we turned out to be.

Do I Want to Know Who You Are?

One night about a year before my mom died, the opportunity to find out about her "secrets" presented itself. At that moment, I decided to not know. She also chose not to tell me. Do I regret the decision? No. Those secrets died with her, and I'm okay with that. Again, you must decide what's right for you. I can't tell you if you'll have regrets later. I can only suggest that you listen to your inner voice. As adults, we can decide what battles we want to fight. We get to determine if that information will hurt or help us.

How do you manage the "who's that" or "who are you?" questions that may appear after your parent(s) die? It depends if you want to or not. And that's your choice. Set a boundary that doesn't allow guilt as a choice. Ask yourself if it's important to you. Then ask why? There are many times when the "why?" is the most essential part of an answer. Remember, it's okay if you don't want to know who those people are. It doesn't make you right, wrong, or anything. It's just a decision. Later, you may change, review, or revise your choices.

REFLECTION OF ONLY YOU   33

We need to remember there are no rules to this life. People do things to us when we're young, and we can't comprehend or change those circumstances. As adults, we get to decide. We can change our minds, go back and do things again, or do them differently. If the other party is willing, we can change everything. It's all about choice, and there will be challenges, too. More than anything else, if things don't quite go as planned, be kind to yourself.

That day I decided to not ask questions, and I have no regrets. I found some information about a previous family in her notes. Perhaps this had been her "secret." I know that if I choose to, I can research online and pursue an extended family. For me, it won't bring any value to my life. I don't automatically think of you as my family because you have the same DNA flowing through your body. I won't suddenly become an excited and loving family member willing to share this new family bond. That's just how I am. You may be different, and that's okay.

I Don't Know You

What do you do if people show up announcing they're your brother or sister? Until it happens, we might be ambivalent. Who is this person? Yes, they bear a resemblance to me, but it doesn't mean I must accept them as members of my family. A friend of mine who grew up with half-siblings continues to investigate the secrets of her family. She has unearthed more half-siblings, stepbrothers, and stepsisters, and thrives on building those new family relationships with these extended families.

I don't feel like that or need to find more family. It is not essential for me. This would only embellish the selfish only-child stereotype for them. As I stated to my best friend one day, what else am I supposed to talk about, the weather, the neighbor's cat? I don't have a husband or significant other, nor kids or grandkids to tell you about, and now I don't have a mom or dad to complain about, either.

I had based who I thought I was and what I needed on my parents. Now, for the first time in my life, the only expectations of me are from me. The only one I'll disappoint is me, which to me, is a novel idea. I haven't even been in the equation for a long time. Where are you in that equation? Do you long for a sibling connection? Do you obsess about finding answers? It's your choice, and the answers may not match your intentions. But you can also change your mind. You need not continue relationships if they aren't suitable for your well-being.

Take some time to assess your mindset and see if it's essential for you to uncover those secrets. First, ensure you're not expecting to resolve a past angst. This person can't heal you. Let's discover how important it is for you. It's okay if you want to pursue it. Or not.

Their Decisions, Not Yours

There are many reasons to get the last will and testament and/ or trust set up before your parent(s) become sick or hospitalized. Perspective can change in a matter of moments when you become immobilized or confined. Decisions like taking out the garbage like you did last week, a simple mundane task, becomes something you long to do.

If your parent(s) complete these documents beforehand, it won't matter if new relatives arrive on your doorstep. Your parent(s) have made their own personal decisions to add the information to those legal documents. It will give you time to discuss their supplications and contemplate how you'll process this new knowledge. You may or may not have had information about these relatives. Don't let what you've seen on TV or in the movies scare you. Yes, I'm sure there can be drama if a prize is worth someone's time and effort, but it's not as frequent as you may think.

You may need to interact with this "new" person. As long as both parties can be adults, interact with them. If they become dramatic and the scene becomes painful, you may find you need to remove yourself and get a third party to oversee the situation. You don't have to take any blame or deal with anything negative concerning this situation. You didn't create it. If you took on those types of responsibilities as a child or young adult, now is the time to let them go.

More than likely, these newfound family members are taking their frustration out on you because they can't take it out on the person with whom they're angry. Don't be that person for them. Be an adult and let them know you're sorry they're having difficulties, but you must deal with other matters. Tell them you wish them well and hope they find peace, and you can reconnect later. Don't become the scapegoat for your parent's personal issues.

Their Issues, Not Yours

After your parents die, one thing you realize is you took on their issues and problems more than you thought. Perhaps you were the dutiful son or the obedient daughter who tried to fix everything to keep the family intact. You're usually so young when you take on their problems as your own that it's impossible to grasp that reality. I did this for a long time, until their last split when my mom packed up and moved several states away, and I left with her. I realized the same focus on them had reappeared a few years before they died.

When they divorced, I was a young adult at the ripe old age of 14. I realized I had issues of my own, which needed my attention, and I didn't care about their problems anymore. Two years later, when I was 16, my best friend was planning to run away from home, so I told her I would go with her. I wasn't running away from anything at my house. I wasn't thinking, "Oh, they don't care about me. They won't even notice I'm gone." I was just the one that came up with the cool idea of, "Hey, I know, let's get a ride and go to California and see the ocean." So we did.

In the two years after their divorce, my parents became involved in their own single lives and less engaged in mine. So, when I talked to my boyfriend two days after my best friend and I left, it shocked me to find out my dad had hired a private detective to look for me. "When did we start caring and worrying about each other? I had places to go, things to do, and I needed to help my friend." (Talking to myself as if I'm an adult in the relationship.) It was as if I had told them, "Sorry, didn't leave a note. Don't worry, remember no news is good news. I'll be back soon." They had no clue where I was or what I was doing most of the time anyway, so I don't think I thought my actions would affect them at all.

CHAPTER 6
THE OTHER FAMILY

When people reach a certain age, they don't want others to tell them what to do. I found this to be true for only-children, regardless of their age. When our parents give us too much freedom, too early, we often do what we want without much regard for others. If we feel guilty about that, it can tip us too far in the opposite direction. Then we care too much.

Sometimes I feel responsible for how others think. People I don't even know. I must pay attention to this and bring it back into balance when needed. I must remind myself I'm not responsible for other people's feelings, not even if they're my parents or relatives. Their emotions are not my responsibility or even my business. By concentrating on what they feel, I neglect my own feelings.

A Plan for Their Pets

Decisions about your parent(s)' pets are another essential consideration. Discuss this with them and pre-plan if possible. Stop reading, put the book down, and go ask them now! Trust me, this will save your heart a lot of pain and grief later.

My dad boarded his 10-year-old, 100-pound German Shepherd at the kennel after entering the hospital. My arrival took a little longer than expected, and there was a sizeable kennel bill to pay. Maggie was also suffering from cancer and several other ailments that would require extensive care and expensive daily medications. I was still trying to wrap my head around caring for my dad, let alone a 100-pound ailing dog too. After talking to the vet, I made the tough decision to put her to sleep.

When my mom first went into the hospital, the next-door neighbor and her best friend took care of her five cats. My mom's best friend stopped on her way home from work to feed and clean litter boxes, and the next-door neighbor checked in on them as needed. I drove the two-and-a-half hours to the hospital and my mom's house as often as I could. I had just started my new job and was still in the probationary period and on-call six days a week. Within two days of my mom's death, these two ladies decided they couldn't manage the feeding, cleaning, and sharing of a schedule between the two of them. I suffered a tidal wave of emotions, and with a lack of choices, I resigned from my job so I could take care of "everything." It would be an understatement to add, "This decision didn't sit well with me."

Five cats. What do you do with five cats? Four that are still feral, even though they are over ten years old, because they've had minimal contact with anyone besides my mom. I had to make a tough decision, and thankfully after several phone calls, the Humane Society agreed to take them. Now to figure out how to get four scared cats from under the bed and into carriers. With my best friend's help, we got them into the carriers, and she earned a new entry on her resume as a "Cat Wrangler." I decided I would adopt the youngest one, who was about two years old. She was more social and didn't spend most of the time under the bed. My mom named her Shadow because she followed my mom around everywhere. A few months after my mom died, it occurred to me, I no longer had my mom, but I had her Shadow.

The Significant Other or Stepparent

Another essential part is your parent's significant other. How do you manage their requests? A significant other is someone your parent didn't marry but perhaps has been in a relationship with for a considerable time. Depending on how long they've been together, several states may establish the union as a common-law marriage. If that's the case, the significant other has certain rights concerning items they've owned together.

The person your parent married after they divorced your other parent may be considered your step-parent. They'll have certain legal rights because of the union. They may be heir to parts of the estate whether or not they're named in the last will and testament. This scenario is where having a last will and testament would be an excellent idea. I suggest getting a lawyer to help you through the process if there's no last will and testament. Also, be aware of the fact you may or may not like this "significant other."

After 20 years together, my mom came home from work one day to find he'd committed suicide in their home. This happened 12 years before she died and affected her mental and physical health for the rest of her life. He was from South Dakota, and his family buried him there. She met more of his family when she went to South Dakota for the funeral and developed relationships with them. These were casual relationships like exchanging holiday and birthday cards, cards announcing new babies, and visiting every three to four years to South Dakota.

The Family of the Significant Other

One day, my mom and I did talk about scattering ashes. She was a little distraught because she didn't have a "place" to scatter her ashes and said she'd never put a lot of thought into it. We talked about my dad's ashes being scattered and how I would like my ashes scattered in Alaska. We talked about her brother, who served in the Navy, and his request that his ashes be scattered off Washington's coast. But our discussion ended there with no real conclusion.

Her significant other's brother and wife kept a winter home in the same city where my mom lived. She was closer to them than the other family members living in South Dakota. I never knew these people. Her bond wasn't my bond. She may have mentioned burying her ashes next to her significant other in South Dakota, but we didn't have an adult conversation about it. Now I was here, the adult only-child, left with the responsibility of taking care of everything after she died. She was no longer there to enforce or make her wishes known.

What her significant other did and how he'd left her didn't sit well with me. She'd suffered from the after-effects of it for 12 years. The end of his suffering had only added to hers. She'd rarely ever lived alone, but after his death, and for the rest of her life, she did.

I Don't Know You and You Don't Know Me

For the duration of my mom's relationship with her significant other, I lived several thousand miles away. I had barely known him. I can still recall how upset she was about being left alone on the day she called to tell me he'd committed suicide. I hadn't forgiven him for leaving her alone. He had abandoned her. To be isolated and alone was a terrible feeling. But I was an only-child and could deal with it better. She wasn't, and it wasn't beneficial to her well-being.

It had been two years since my dad died, which at the time was my most significant emotional hurdle. I had only just made it past that hurdle and was rebuilding my life again, and then my mom died. She was the only thing left defining who I thought I was, the last thing connected to me. Even though it was only the ashes of a body she didn't inhabit anymore, it was still her. I had to admit, I also wanted to keep her all to myself. It hadn't occurred to me that this was the first time I had her all to myself since I was 13. Could this be the reason I didn't want to ship her ashes to South Dakota? How was it supposed to be okay to hand her ashes over to someone I didn't know or think of as family?

I made the phone call to the significant others' brother and told him I would like him to take her ashes to South Dakota. This man who sat in front of me didn't know me. He knew me as the daughter who hadn't spoken to her mom for years. The one who he'd heard stories about causing her mom heartache and tears. There was no acknowledgment of every story having two sides and that it had been in my best interest to limit contact with her.

Did I want to send her ashes to South Dakota? No, I didn't. Was I pressured by the brother of the significant other? Yes, I did. He thought he knew what she wanted. I believed I would be a terrible daughter if I didn't do it. It shouldn't have mattered what he thought of me. I sometimes forget that what others think of me is not my business. As someone who has strived for everyone to like me -- and most have -- letting what they think of me affect my life decisions is where I get off track. This was one of those instances where I couldn't find my "adult." My grief and how much I missed my mom was blinding me. I couldn't vocalize my feelings or that I needed more time.

I tried to find the best path for the whole situation to not affect or negatively reflect on me. I put on the act of the polite little adult. The one I learned to be when I was a child. I didn't know this person, but I agreed and smiled at him as I handed him the box with her ashes. He wasn't family to me, and I wasn't family to him. I acted like I had everything under control; my feelings, this situation, in fact, the whole situation. Everything was fine, right?

The situation wasn't pleasant, but I got through it well enough. As you'll find in this process, there will be many things you either wish you did differently or had asked for more time to process. I didn't know these people, and they didn't know me. They may have heard my mom's side of the story about our relationship, but they weren't interested in me. They didn't care about the last two years my mom and I spent together. That time had healed a lot of wounds on both sides.

A few months later, I found pages she had written about when her significant other committed suicide and how it affected her. That was when I realized I had learned from my mom, the skill of acting like everything was fine when it wasn't fine at all. It was a skill she'd perfected. In those pages, she stated she wanted her ashes placed next to his in South Dakota. She also mentioned how she'd done an excellent job of making everyone think she'd been okay for 12 years. But she hadn't been okay. She missed him immensely, and she was never brave enough, or mentally well enough, to have another intimate relationship in her life again.

In circumstances like this, people may characterize me as cold. Have you seen this version of you show up in a situation like this? The opinions I expressed kept me safe from what I was feeling about this decision. But I wouldn't visit a gravesite, even if it was just around the corner. I bought the headstone and shipped it to South Dakota, and they placed it beside her significant other's and buried her ashes there. They set the headstone and texted me a photo, and I've never heard from the brother again.

Have Those Conversations

How can we consider the subject of death from a distinct perspective that will help everyone? Not addressing it doesn't make it go away. It's always hanging around in the background, taking up energy. By acknowledging it, we can bring it into a space where it's safe to discuss it, and we can feel safer when the time comes to deal with those responsibilities. With no one to ask, though, it can be tough not knowing what to do and dealing with grief.

When I opened my mom's briefcase, if I had known what she wanted, there would've only been a slight twinge of rebelliousness. I would still have those feelings toward her significant other. But there would've been no doubt what she wanted, and it could've saved me from that experience. I still would've kept a small urn of ashes for myself, but I would've been okay with giving the rest of them to a stranger. I wasn't able or willing to see his feelings for her or for his brother. All I saw was she wasn't his mom, and he didn't empathize with me or my situation.

Even if he didn't think of me as a horrible person, it didn't matter overall, and I shouldn't put it into the mix. But the adult only-child wasn't there during those moments to have those rational adult thoughts. Have those conversations. Ask your parent(s) to talk to you about what they want. Use an example from their life about when one of their parents or a sibling died. Using an example, they can relate to what may help them see the worth of doing this now and not later. They will realize it'll hurt less to talk about it now and will help you so much more later.

CHAPTER 7
DEATH ISN'T CHEAP

People die. Then the "older and wiser" ones stepped in, took charge, and did what they needed to do. Did they have magic wands? I never heard them talk about the process of having a burial or cremation or what happened to the person's belongings. I didn't realize the costs associated with death or how you took care of those things. There were always three or four relatives who took care of those things, and after the funeral, the journey of life continued.

But now there was only me. I had missed the class on what you do when people die, and I was getting a "figure it out as you go" education. Because I already did many things alone, I realized that was the only way you could survive doing it alone. It was one of those times the strength which came from being an only-child humbled me. Did other people, people who had siblings or other close family ties, have this strength? I seemed to own it just as naturally as having brown hair.

I wanted a swing set when I was six years old, so my dad helped me save my pennies, and when I had enough, we went to the Western Auto store to buy it. A swing set is so much easier to put together if you get the instructions (and follow them … yes, that's helpful too). Can you put it together without them? Sure! But it'll take you more time to complete the task. My dad was never a follow-the-instruction-sheet kind of guy. But I was.

At that moment, when I needed to decide whether to have a burial or cremation, I wished for an instruction sheet, a magic wand, something, anything, that could give me more than the question mark I was holding. That information would have empowered me, and I wouldn't question, or second-guess, or listen to people who would be gone two days later. In fact, I hadn't known those people two days ago. Don't listen to them. You aren't obligated to anyone, except your physical, mental, and spiritual health and the respect for your parent(s).

They didn't include the instructions I had hoped for, and you may not have them, either. Do what you believe is right in your heart, and try not to second-guess them later. Although you're going to, no worries, it's normal. I had my dad's ashes split in thirds (who knew you could do that? Not me, until I asked). The story I created in my mind was that he wanted his ashes in three places, and he would've stated that in those instructions.

If you're not sure and you've no one to ask, then stop reading and go to a calm and peaceful place and ask yourself what you think they would tell you. If you don't come up with anything, then do what you would like someone to do with your ashes. I'll cover more about this in a later section.

Cremation: Their Ashes

Did anyone tell you about the ashes? Did any of your other relatives get cremated? Again, it's one of those things people just don't discuss. You have no idea what to do with this box you picked up from the funeral home if you didn't take part in the process of someone else's cremation. I didn't. Now, what do you do? A little warning, there are more ashes than you might think.

My cousin told me about a place in Tennessee that my Dad had mentioned to her several times. Our descendants had settled there when they first came to America. It sounded like a place where my dad would've liked his ashes scattered. I asked my cousin if she would take a third of his ashes there for me. She was familiar with the place, and agreed. Later that year, she sent me photos of the area where she'd scattered his ashes and a heartfelt poem she wrote about the experience.

I spread another third of his ashes around the home he'd lived in for the last 30 years, a place I knew had made him happy. The vet had given me a keepsake plaster cast of his dog Maggie's footprint. She'd been his sole companion for the last 10 years of his life, so I broke that into pieces and added it to his ashes. I wandered around the property, letting the wind carry the ashes, and I just talked to him. It rained that night, soaking the ashes and memories into the ground. For me, it was a sign. It was a pat on the back for a job well done and a thank you from my dad.

I asked another cousin to take the last third back to the city where my dad was born and raised. Most of his life had taken place there, and it was where I had also been born and spent my first 14 years. His first wife was buried there in the 1950's in the family plot. She was the first love of his life (after his mom), and again I thought this would be a place he would want his ashes scattered. I didn't know you couldn't just go scatter someone's ashes at a cemetery plot. The staff there told me there were no spaces left in the original plot, but they could place any other ashes or bodies in a nearby mausoleum.

I inquired about the cost, and I still shake my head at the fees they charge. Death isn't cheap. Like the cremation, it had a set price. I asked them if there was any way to reduce the cost, they told me the only possibility would be a military benefit. He had been in the military, but not long enough to qualify for any burial benefits. There may be benefits available if your parent was in the military or was a first responder. Check with the Veteran's Administration in your state and the public service office where they served. I needed to consider this in the context that there was no family left except a few cousins and me, and we would all die within the next 10 to 20 years. After that, there was no one who would visit a gravesite.

Their Ashes, Your Feelings

Have you heard those aphorisms about how girls are dads' favorite, and boys are moms' favorite? For the child, I think it's the one you see yourself reflected in the most. It's the one we connect with on that profound level and compare ourselves to the most. It's the one we wanted to emulate and sometimes the one we tried our hardest not to imitate.

Somewhere within my stages of grieving, I realized how possessive I had been of them. It is one of those things that's so intrinsic to your being an only-child, you don't even know it's there until it's not. It cleared up murky events and timeframes when I wasn't sure why things had gone wonky between myself and them. I was an adult; I made my own choices, and I had for a long time, at least I thought I did.

The rebellious side of me kept a small amount of my mom's ashes. It was like saying to the brother of my mom's significant other, "Okay, fine, I'll do what you want, but I'm keeping a bit of her for me." I have her ashes in a small urn that I carry in my purse, and I know she's always with me. It's not her, but in my mind, it's the essence of her, and I may never let her go. The best thing is, I realize now I don't have to, and it's okay if I don't.

I didn't experience the same attachment to my dad's ashes. I hadn't been contending with anyone over where to scatter them or disputing about who had knowledge of my parent's last wishes. When I sprinkled the third of my dad's ashes around his yard and gave the other thirds to my cousins to spread in the proper places, I didn't feel a need to keep any of them. All I experienced was freedom. When they cremated my dad, the facility put a numbered emblem in with the body for identification. The funeral home had attached it to the outside of the box that held his ashes. That emblem is my connection to him.

What surprises me most is I wasn't aware I would feel this way. I didn't see my mom for more than 15 years -- on purpose. I had even visited the city where she lived several times during those years but had not told her I was there. It was what was best for me. I recognized this was true because I don't regret it or consider that I lost time with her; it was time I needed to heal and try to find myself by myself -- with as little influence as possible from her.

During those last two years of her life after my dad died, the time I spent with her allowed her to see me from a different perspective. She had still thought of me as a 20-year-old; she had spent little time with me, the responsible adult. To be fair, my parents had no clue about a lot of what happened to me or what I had done since I was nine years old, even when I lived under their roofs.

Tough Decisions which Only You Can Make

What obligations do you feel you owe the deceased and the remaining family? You'll need to figure this out. What do your finances allow you to undertake? What can you manage right now? Figure out what's right for you. Your parent(s) has died, and you can respect their memory, but you shouldn't experience shame or guilt about what you can or can't do. You'll need those funds to get yourself back on your feet.

For me, I had given up everything except for my belongings. I had no job or life to go back to, and it was going to take a generous amount of funds just to facilitate the move. I had to figure out where I was going, what I would grow up to be this time, and I'd need those funds to figure it out. You may find yourself in a situation like mine where there wasn't a lot of time to spend thinking about those things, so give yourself a bit of time, if possible, and permission to befriend yourself.

These are those times you can be reticent and listen to the suggestions or advice another relative gives you in the matters at hand. Always keep in mind, though, it's your decision. You've got the burden of that decision, and it'll be heaviest on you, even more so if you're by yourself. They can disagree with you. But everyone should respect you and the position you're in, having to make these decisions on your own. It's not about whether it's your right or what you deserve. What matters is that you're there, and you're making the tough decisions.

You may find that you need to let go of the fact the people may not do something you entrusted them to do as you asked or may not do it at all. It may leave you feeling the person disrespected your choices and they don't identify with your burden of responsibility. They don't realize the balance you had to strike between what you thought your parent(s) may have wanted and what you could do. I don't control whether the other parties completed the wishes I asked them to do. It's their burden to bear, not my worry. It'll do you well to remember that, too.

Be consistent with yourself. It's okay if the people who surround you don't understand you. Because unless they're an only-child, they won't understand. Don't let those with siblings tell you how easy it is for you because you don't have to contend with brothers or sisters. They can't fathom what it's like to be an only-child any more than you know what it's like to have siblings. We all have our own circumstances and people we must accommodate or, at least, be respectful to. If you can't be polite, then take a break from that person. It's okay to do that. Later they may find the discernment they don't have now.

CHAPTER 8
WHOSE VOICE IS THIS?

My inner only-child was screaming, "How did this happen? What can I do? This sucks! I hate this! Why, why, why, why?" But, really, it was the silence that got me. How did I miss their voice(s) crowded in with mine? It had seemed so natural it never occurred to me, they shouldn't be there, let alone be that loud? It's the person with no remaining connections to anyone by blood or by love who sits alone, wondering, *What's important? What's the reason?* You question the norms.

Our parents didn't engage in those conversations with us. Did they just figure we would come to take care of things? They didn't seem to worry about it, but I've no way to verify that. I guess their lack of action could be fear. Their lack of talking with us shows fear. Is it a fear of dying? I don't think so. We all know it's inevitable. We see it all the time; you can smoke, drink, and do many other things that are bad for your health, and you could still live to be 90 old or die at 55. There's no formula or rules that seem to pertain to this life. You can do all the right things in life and not live forever, thank goodness!

Our parents viewed death and funerals through the lenses of their parents or relatives. For their parents, cremation wasn't the norm for that generation. The norm was to get a casket and then put the dead body out on display for all to see. My guess is they did this, so you believed they had died, even though the person in the casket rarely resembled how they appeared in actual life. But that was the norm. You spent thousands of dollars and put the body in the ground. They would take flowers and visit the cemeteries on the anniversary of their death and put them on the grave, and they would beat themselves up when they didn't get around to doing that. Time changes what one generation thinks is necessary concerning many things, even about death.

Your Fears

What are your biggest fears about the death of your parents? Take a little time to figure out what you believe about it and why. It doesn't matter what the why is, but what matters is that you're aware of it. You'll need to examine it closer and search deeper for a reason. Is it the best decision for you? What types of things am I wondering about aloud?

I'm talking about taking on the responsibility of your parent's hospitalization, home-care, property, pets, and obligations for their ashes or body after they die. Is it just assumed you are the person? We don't discuss it. I get it. I wouldn't want the person I was hoping to care for me to turn me down, either. Even though the adult in me would comprehend they weren't turning me down as a person, it would still hurt. Perhaps it would be in the best interest of both parties to delegate someone else and find an additional person who can support the primary person. It's tough to make those decisions by yourself and not have anyone to talk to about them.

It's helpful to have one parent who can help you after the other parent passes. Or will you be the resilient one for the grieving parent and have no time or strength to care for your own emotions? It's essential to find support and time to care for yourself, too. This is important for your well-being and your grieving parent as well.

It's not magic. Those feelings don't disappear. Getting through that time is a process I've had a tough time admitting, even now. Note, though, I didn't say grief was an exact process. It's individual for each person, and it can be similar to what others go through, but it'll be your own experience. Although you may relate better to the experience of another adult only-child. Someone who has siblings will have a different family system perspective. Their relationship with those siblings and their parents isn't the same as those of the only-child.

The most important question to ask yourself is, "Do I want the responsibility?" The first time a therapist asked me that question, I didn't have an answer other than, "No, but who else is going to do it?" and "I don't have a choice, I'm the only-child, isn't it just expected of me?" Yes, it had been, but we had never had an adult conversation about it. I had a choice; I just didn't have a voice at the time to make my feelings about the situation known to my parents.

What's Stopping You?

What's stopping you from broaching the topic? If it's fear, remember it'll be a thousand times more difficult if you're experiencing a lot of resentment about something you didn't want to do. Ask them to spend time on this now. Do it soon. Remember, just listen. This is the time to listen and acknowledge their last wishes, but it's also the time to discuss them with each other as adults. Make plans for another family member to do it if you believe you can't care for them. Or find someone who can be in your place when the time comes time to carry out those wishes.

Do what you can for now. If you can't do what your parent requested, it's okay to do what you can with your resources. I didn't know what would happen or how I would deal with everything when my parents ended up in the hospital before they died. My dad was 3,000 miles away; I had to uproot my life and go, and I had no way of knowing when, or if, I would ever return to that life. There was no one to stay behind and take care of things where I was living so I could leave and take care of my dad and come back. I didn't like it, and it buried me in resentment, but I didn't know what else to do.

The only thing I discerned was I wasn't comfortable stepping back and giving those responsibilities to someone else. Which meant I had to pack up and go, even though it also meant giving up my life. It took me more than two years to regain a sense of it. To retrieve a sense of accomplishment and stability. To know that I could still take care of myself, and I could roll on and meet the next challenges. I got a decent-paying job and moved a few hours away from where my mom lived, and then six weeks later, she died. For the second time in my life, something I had known was inevitable happened.

This time, though, I didn't live so far away, but the timing was unfortunate. I had a better idea this time of what I had to do after having dealt with my dad's death. Except I had more to take care of this time. This time, I also didn't have her or anyone else to be on the phone with me every day — someone to help me get through it all. I kept the new apartment I had just moved into and didn't move back to the city. Overall, it would be the best decision I made for myself.

What You Think They Know About You

I loathe going to hospitals; I don't do well in that environment. Nope, not one bit. My body senses everything that is filtering through the air. The pain, sickness, fear, stress from the hospital staff, and emotions from the patients' family members: I am aware of all of it. It's a crushing weight upon me when I enter a hospital, get in an elevator, walk down hallways, and pick up all the noises of conversations and machines.

It doesn't help that everyone I've ever known who went into a hospital didn't come out. In my mind, it's the last stop, the last station, and it's a painful place for me. I disassociate, and I'm not present. When a crucial decision is at hand, I won't be fully present. If you were aware of those things about me, would you choose me to be the one who oversees your care within that facility? At those times, when you can't make those decisions for yourself, or it may be in your best interest for others to make those decisions for you, would you want me to make them? I wouldn't.

Then my question becomes, "Did my parents know this about me?" I'm not sure. If we had discussed their last wishes, we could've discovered this and found a better plan. I don't know if I'll ever believe I did what was best for my parents when they were in the hospital. Part of me says, "It's okay. It was how things had to happen. Otherwise, something would've intervened."

I want to believe the decisions I made were right, and the things I didn't figure out until later wouldn't have changed the outcome. One harsh reality of this situation is you can't go back and fix anything. You can't take something out to put something in that's new and better. Those are not options. There is nothing anyone can do differently. The space is empty, and you can't revisit it. For someone like me who hates to give up, I still catch my mind trying to fix it and make a different result appear.

But it doesn't. It's just the same space, that same empty space. I share these things not for you to feel sorry for me or pity me, but to give you a reason to have these talks with your parent(s) now when it can help everyone! Is it a fail-safe plan? No, but at least I would know of another option, and if I didn't feel comfortable or if it weren't okay, I wouldn't have to do it, at least not by myself.

Have those tough conversations. Take the difficulty out of those situations that will come later. If you have them now, you will show each other a level of respect as human beings who may not be as strong as you think. Did I step up when the time came? Yes, I did. Did I give it all I had? Yes, and then a little more. Did I do it out of love? I don't know; it seemed more like a duty, a responsibility, than feeling love for them. Having those earlier conversations could've ensured what I did was out of the love I had for them.

Your Values, Not Theirs

Now is the time to put this book down and figure out what's important to you with burials and funerals and ask yourself, "Are these my values or someone else's?" Are they your parent's values, or perhaps your grandparent's values? If you didn't have a path laid out for handling your parent(s) death, it's okay to bring your principles into the situation. You can't ask them, but trust in yourself that you have the sense to oversee this respectfully.

What's important to you? Is it essential you bury your family member in a "place?" If you have a funeral, how many family members would attend? Having a funeral may guilt others to travel thousands of miles, which may burden them. Did your parent or parents have an extended period of hospitalization? How many times did this family member call, visit, ask, or speak to you? Did they offer anything, even if it was an ear to listen? If your answer is zero, then please don't feel obligated to include this person or their wishes in your decisions. If they weren't there before your parent(s) died, then they can work it out on their own time without complicating your grief.

What's important? Are you okay with the cremation process? If not, that's okay. No one should judge you. They're not dealing with the loss of the person from whom you gained a sense of yourself. It's possible they loved and shared some of this person's life. They might be a sibling who would be the closest to the same relationship. But overall, the relationship between a parent and the only-child is a unique thing. I used to speculate that I was the only unusually unique thing about our family unit. It wasn't until those parts detached that I realized we had been a cohesive unit. There was always a sense of them in my world, even when we felt estranged.

When I was writing this manuscript, I often put the word "passed" instead of "died." I kept going back and correcting it, and I'll edit it out before I publish the book, except for this passage. I realized I was using it to soften the fact they had "died." But it wasn't helping. It was just prolonging the truth.

Perhaps it's a sign you're healing and able to accept it. If you believe you'll see them again, this can be a pleasant thought or an awful thought, or one with mixed blessings. In the beginning, you have lots of questions, questions for them, questions for God, or your version of God. You'll have questions for and about everyone.

I haven't decided if it's an amenable thing or not because I'm not sure it's a "thing" at all. Nobody on this planet knows what happens to you when you die. No matter what color your skin is, how much money you have, your religion, the language you speak, the customs you follow, the beliefs you hold -- it's all just theories and speculations. We don't know. No definite proof exists.

I infer this is hidden from us on purpose. Consider how we've manipulated the birth process, something that's much easier for us to study. We even control what we've presumed we know about death. Consider the study of cryogenics, which is the scientific process of freezing and storing a person's body after death. People take the chance that scientific research will discover a way to bring them back to life later. They don't have that answer, but they believe science could one day be successful.

We know the physical processes. But we don't know what happens when the last bit of oxygen leaves our breath, when our heart stops beating, and our senses cease recording into our mind the memories and effects of life. Science still hasn't interpreted everything about what happens to us when we sleep --the time when our conscious minds are not aware of our bodies. When it keeps doing what it's so adequate at doing. What a wonderfully built machine! Science doesn't fully know why we dream, either. Where do all those images come from that roam through our minds? Are they real or imagined? There are so many things we don't know, but the looming unanswered question is, "What happens to us after we die?"

Who I Am

Recently, someone asked me, "What major event or situation made you who you are today?" My answer was, "I was an only-child." It shaped my beliefs more than anything else. What about you? Even though other events in my life weren't pleasant and had left a mark on me, nothing was as profound as being an only-child. And even considering all the unpleasant things, I wouldn't change it.

That perspective comes with age and experiencing life. I trust I've also gotten better at forgiving people, and learning that holding on to past hurts will only hurt me. I can't change events from long ago. What happened didn't crush me. The fact is, it strengthened me. Was it pleasant? No. Do I wish my parents would've paid more attention? Yes, of course. But those things also changed me and influenced who I am, too.

The comment, *blood is thicker than water*, has no real meaning for me. As an only-child, I didn't seem to have any experiences to connect to how people were using it. Sometimes they used it in a way that made me feel left out. You know, it's like the time you were at your friend's house for the holiday. Their uncle, who only shows up once in a blue moon, rallied the family together, declaring, "Even though sometimes we don't get along, this family means more to me than anyone! Because you know, blood is thicker than water!!"

To me, it meant I lacked something, which seemed essential and valued. Then there was the time when I was at my cousin's house. The six of them, three brothers and three sisters, who seemed to squabble over everything and fought, got mad, and cried. Their dad made a comment to rally them together, exclaiming, they all "Loved each other regardless of how much they fought because blood was thicker than water." Even though I had the same blood, I didn't sense being a part of the larger group. I didn't understand why I thought I lacked something or didn't feel I was part of that family group. I had no context to grasp.

By the time I was an adult, I had contemplated that overall, the thought of my "family" hadn't had been a pleasant concept for me, neither my actual family nor my married family. They had grand expectations of me that even my perfectionist ways couldn't meet. Which still surprised me because I expected so much from myself. My sixth-grade teacher wrote on my report card, "She always does more than is expected of her." Why was a 12-year-old concerned with that? And what expectations did a 12-year-old have? Were the expectations of those around me different from my expectations?

As a young adult, did adults think of you as older? Did you ever notice that or get the impression that the adults, or even you, thought you understood things you didn't? Did you wish you had a sibling or someone else to take the focus off you as the one to meet the needs of your parent(s) and anyone else around you? That sometimes, you made those teenage adult decisions based on what you had seen an adult do? You used what you saw them do without knowing the complete story about this person or having a full realization of the adult actions you were copying.

Your Answers

I don't have a conclusive answer for how you'll deal with the loss when your parent dies. I struggled with all those questions. What is it that really mattered? What was I supposed to be doing with my life? Was I doing it? Was I okay with what I was doing? I had an extraordinary sense of my working self and what I could do. Many only-children have multiple skills and talents and do well in many occupations. Find the place in your life where you felt the strongest and the most secure. Gather yourself from that place and sustain yourself.

You'll survey all the stuff and belongings your parent(s) left behind and wonder, *This can't be what it's all about.* You'll find items they should've tossed in the trash but held onto for various reasons. Reasons you will never know. You'll scrutinize the stuff you own and try to unearth a specific meaning from it all. I like pretty things and pictures, and I have lots of eye-candy in my space. On certain days it energizes me, inspires me, and brings me joy. Other days I consider having a massive yard. All this stuff will end up just being a headache for someone else who won't behold these items through my eyes or have the memories I've attached to them.

When you go through your parent's belongings after they die, you'll get a sense of what they treasured. You may find items that belonged to their parents or items that belonged to their siblings. Your parents may have cherished these items. You'll also find things they never dealt with, and instead, stuffed into a box for a later time.

I found items like the boxes and boxes of papers and check stubs from my father's business dating from 1968 until 1982 when it closed. He put in many hours there, after he'd put in many longer and more demanding hours at his other job as a firefighter. My mom also spent many hours working at the business. As a child, that's where I had spent my weekends and summers. When I was no longer content with being sequestered in my dad's tiny corner office by myself, watching B-movies and Saturday morning cartoons, I started working there, too. You could say it was my first job. I was about 11 years old, and I would answer phones, take orders, and look up parts for customers. Perhaps I could help with the business, too, since this was a significant source of strife in my parent's life, and it always had a seat at our dinner table each night.

My dad had never dealt with his feelings around the loss of his business or his family. The last time my mom packed up and left him, I went with her. Perhaps it was too much for him. It wasn't just a reminder of what he had but also of what he'd lost. He went bankrupt and closed the business a few years after my mom and I left. I spent days shredding those papers and receipts. I had to sift through it all in case he had put something valuable in the boxes on purpose or by accident.

As I spent those hours shredding and fussing at my dad for not doing something with them before now, I realized I was dealing not only with my feelings about them but his feelings about them, too. Much later, I found purpose in that task, which had irritated me so much. It's surprising how unrelated things can end up causing growth for us.

CHAPTER 9
WHAT ARE YOUR THOUGHTS ON DEATH?

Most people have experienced seeing death, even if they only saw it in a movie or a television program. What do you think happens to you when you die? Are you comfortable thinking of that and your answers? If you're the only one left in your family, you may also ponder, *What's the point?* Even if they bury you, no one will visit your grave, and yes, something is sad about that.

I consider burying people an outdated convention kept alive by the funeral companies. I understand it's a lucrative business, but I feel they need to modernize and change with the times and not promote this outdated system. Putting dead bodies in boxes in the ground continues to consume land that could be used for affordable housing or another needed commodity. You can honor loved ones who died in ways that don't involve spending thousands or tens of thousands of dollars to give them a high-dollar makeover, put them into a fancy box with silky cushions, and then place it six feet under the ground. These gravesites are often many miles away from where the family lives, negating visits from them.

Your Last Wishes

Have you thought about your last wishes and what you would like to happen when you die? Not only is taking care of your parents' last wishes and the legalities essential, but it's also necessary to take care of your last wishes. "Who will decide my care if I can't?" I still struggle with this. It's a daunting subject for me to contemplate. I can't discuss this with any children or a significant other, and it's hard to put this responsibility on a friend, knowing they would be alone making these decisions.

Even if I write my wishes down, although it makes them more probable, I've no guarantee it'll happen that way. I circle back to if it even matters. Because it's also possible, there won't be a friend close enough to carry out my last wishes. It could be a stranger who finds you and your stuff unattended by life anymore. That's a challenging thought. It's not one you want to go too deeply into, especially if the loss of your parent(s) was recent. Don't put too much on yourself, no matter how strong you think you are; this is too sobering a topic.

I struggle with the "who" and whether it's important. Because I won't be here, I won't worry about it, at least not in my version of heaven. I'll leave behind all the worries. The things I consider necessary will have no bearing because they won't be where I am. After I die, I won't know how everything turns out, what happens to my body, or anything related to me or my belongings. So, does it matter who gets my stuff?

I struggle more with "what am I to do with the rest of my life?" If you've lost both of your parents, you may feel this, too. My realization was acute after my mom died. This feeling of not knowing who I was without them, of not having anyone to connect to, for the first time in my life.

So much of what I had done in my life had been to make them proud. Doing the things I thought would make them pleased to tell others I was their daughter. I had done a few things for myself, but the majority had been to get recognition from them. I wasn't even aware of this, and they had no way of knowing I needed that acknowledgment from them. As an adult, we realize we can't blame them, and we need to let go of our fear of disappointing them.

Making your Plans

This will be more challenging than making their plans, asking about them, or any of the earlier stuff we've discussed. They had someone to leave it to, someone to take responsibility for them and their property. First, examine what you have and decide what could be of value to someone else. Make a list of those items. If you have someone you would like to have them or a place you want to give them, then legalize those plans.

I find I'm getting better with my feelings surrounding having no immediate family or heirs, and I worry about it less and less. It would be beneficial to pass some of my belongings to someone or a place that means something to me. I need to be a responsible steward and follow the advice I give others. The paperwork and legal documents need to be in place. I remind myself I want to be the one to complete the plans and make those choices. Otherwise, the state will make those choices for me.

For me, it's my best friend's first grandson. She has a close relationship with him, and although I don't share those same maternal feelings, I decided I would leave anything I have of value to him. I'm giving it to him because I hope it'll be a blessing and help him start something he wouldn't be able to do otherwise. I've discussed this with my friend. She knows she's the beneficiary of my accounts, and I gave her that information. She also knows my wish to leave those funds to her grandson. My second choice would be a church that I attend or one that could benefit from the bequest.

Do you need a Plan B?

Put Plan A in place first before making a backup plan. It's of no use to have two plans that are both incomplete. What if you don't have anyone to give your belongings? Well, you can leave everything as is and believe it'll work out like it should or take the time to complete a plan if it's significant to you. Have the conversations with the people you need to and get the legal papers completed to facilitate your wishes. Then forget about it. It's no longer a worry.

Can you see that not having a plan is the precise scenario that continues to be stressful and cause worry for you and your parent(s) if they're still alive? Even if they don't verbalize it, they worry about those things. Maybe they're waiting for you to approach them to discuss these things, perhaps not. When plans are being made for their belongings and property, don't hold off because you assume you'll have time later. Those unexpected events are more likely to occur when they are getting upwards in age. My mom had just turned 80 a few weeks before she died.

My mom and I had decided not to change the house's title, making me a joint owner because we were in the middle of plans to move her into a different home. Waiting wasn't a sound idea because the unexpected in life was about to happen. Not having my name on the title wasn't too problematic since I was the heir for the property in the will. It could've become a significant worry and a lot more legal paperwork if I hadn't gotten the last will and testament completed. We all suppose we can do it tomorrow, right? Don't let it be something you wished you did yesterday, for yourself or for them.

I'll forever always thank God for giving me strength that day to complete my mom's last will and testament. For not letting me give up or push it aside again for one more day. It was imperative to bring the resources and people together that day. Later that day, when things started getting harder and harder, and it wasn't working out, I just kept pushing even when the people who had agreed to come weren't sure they were coming. There was a voice in my head, an unseen hand that kept nudging me forward. I had to get it done; I just had to, and because I persisted, it came together just like an orchestrated play.

That afternoon when everyone arrived at the hospital, my mom was awake, talking to people, and her coloring had improved. There was a grace about her as she signed the last document to hold her initials and signatures. It was the best thing I could've accomplished for me since I had no idea that in two days, she would no longer be there.

CHAPTER 10
WHAT TO DO WITH ALL THEIR STUFF

What's this? And why did they keep this? Geez! There will be lots of those items, if a) you didn't have the "what to do with me and my stuff" conversation, and b) if they hadn't dealt with things from their lives, or c) they didn't have the ability or energy to do an efficient house cleaning. I think this could be an agreeable habit for all of us. Going through the things we own and making sure we haven't just stuffed items into boxes to go through later. Although there will be items like that. And it's okay. Just try to limit this if possible, and every now and then, take inventory of your stuff.

Burden of Stuff

Treasures and mementos will get buried under other things. Many things will get mingled together. You'll forget what item belonged to whom or why you kept something. You'll remember a few items you wished you hadn't thrown away and forget stuff you threw out or gave away. I found many things I recognized that belonged to my mom's mother. She also had several items that had belonged to her dad. Some of these items were already 50 years old when she inherited them, and then she'd kept them for almost 50 more years.

My mom had deemed these were the objects she couldn't part with, even though she hadn't seen them in a long time. It was just like the items I kept that belonged to my parents. I imagined she had experienced comfort and closeness to her parents from those items, too. She didn't have their ashes. She had buried her parents in cemeteries in different states thousands of miles from where she lived, and she'd rarely visited their gravesites to add the requisite flowers on the anniversaries of their deaths.

There's a burden that comes along with all that stuff. You want to keep everything, but you know you can't keep it all. When I sorted through my parent's belongings, there wasn't a lot of time to decide this, nor the space to keep things, nor the will to figure out how to keep them. In both instances, I gave away more than I kept, and sometimes I've chastised myself for making such quick decisions on several items: "I shouldn't have given that to so and so, or I shouldn't have thrown that away." Sometimes I stop and give myself a pep talk and remember it's only stuff, and if I need the money, it'll come to me. Berating myself for things I can't change doesn't help me grow.

In the long run, none of it matters. It's okay, and I will remind myself again and again: I couldn't keep it all, it's okay. The items I kept are things to which I am sentimentally attached. After I die, the person responsible for my things will have other thoughts about them, or maybe have no thoughts at all. To them, most of it'll just be stuff.

Don't Be So Hard on Yourself

I gave away so many of my dad's belongings because I wanted to leave South Carolina as soon as possible. I had lived there for 21 years, and from the moment I arrived, I never wanted to be there. Eight years later, I had adjusted more after getting married, making friends, and securing gainful employment.

Thirteen years after that, when an opportunity presented itself to move somewhere else that was too amazing to pass up, I did, even though it was an arduous undertaking involving a 3,000-mile journey. It would be seven more years after that before I would realize I had been oblivious to the hovering, protective father who had lived across the street from me for 15 years.

Before I moved away, it seemed I was just waiting for him to die so I could move somewhere else, and it didn't sit right with me. If he lived for another 20 years, I didn't want to resent him for that and use the resentment to blame him for my unhappiness because I didn't move when I had this opportunity. I'd figure out how to handle the situation if he got sick and couldn't care for himself or died when it happened. There was no way to know how challenging that task would be when the time came or that I would deal with most of it by myself.

A few months after I moved, I learned that my dad watched me come and go to my job on their parking lot's webcam. He was keeping track of me even when I was 3,000 miles away. Why? Was he protective? Or overprotective? A few family members on my dad's side disagreed with my moving so far away. They thought I abandoned him. I asked him if he wanted to go with me, but he told me he wasn't interested in moving and leaving his home.

He was healthy, although he was overweight. He'd smoked for more than 50 years, and when he quit, food replaced the cigarettes. In the 21 years I lived there, I had only known of him going to the doctor once. One year he broke out in shingles, and by the time he let me know, it was so bad I had to take him to urgent care. He didn't take any prescription medications because he said he didn't want to be like his relatives, who had to take handfuls of pills multiple times a day. Unless it was an emergency, he didn't go to a doctor.

It was his choice and what he wanted. It wasn't my right to tell him he had to do something he didn't want to do, and I still feel that way. I don't think the drugs they pumped into him during his stay in the hospital were beneficial to his overall health. There is no doubt the interesting conversations we had in the emergency room, when he told me things I know he wouldn't have told me otherwise, happened because he was on drugs!

Give it Away

Even though I've had times I wished I had made better or different decisions, give away as much as you can. Most of those decisions I made were under the pressure of a self-imposed time constraint or implied financial decision. Make the choice of whether you need to take time now to sell those items and put the money toward rebuilding your life. Give yourself a little time if you can. Especially if you are in a situation like mine after my dad died, when I wasn't even sure what my life looked like, let alone a restored version of it. If you give it away with a giving heart, I believe it will come back to you in abundance later. So give it away.

You may spend money to store the items and sell them later. Remember, it will negate any money you could have made on the item if you keep them in storage for too long. You want to avoid paying for storage for things you don't need and won't keep, anyway. Try looking at the situations from a fresh perspective. If like me, you're a perfectionist, it's natural for us to second-guess our decisions because you think you can always do better than what you did. I'm learning not to devalue myself because I failed to be my version of perfect. Instead, I regard what I've done and find the value in it. Give it away. More than likely, you'll be okay with it later on.

A Starting Point

What's the first step? Where do you start? Are there things already in place? Start with something simple. It will be a challenge, but it will help you to get started. You will do a lot of things on autopilot, and that's okay. What is your timeline? Are there things you need to do and decide right away? Find out what decisions your parent(s) made and what's in place. The decision about burial or cremation is the most important. It will be helpful to know this information as soon as possible.

Remember the sympathetic people I told you about at the hospital and funeral home? They are the ones who can answer your questions about burial or cremation. If you're not sure if your parent(s) set anything up and you don't know what to do, contact me. I can help you brainstorm and discover your options based on the area where you live. It makes it easier to decide what you're okay with when you have a clear picture of your options.

In the town where my dad lived, a burial plot next to his sister was available. But I didn't want to take on the responsibility and costs associated with a funeral. It would involve buying a casket, placing it in the ground, and paying the funeral home and staff fees. There were specific honors that could occur because he had been in the military and a firefighter.

As much as I thought he would appreciate those things, I wouldn't find any comfort attending a funeral with only a few relatives or friends. Do what's right for you, even if you don't feel absolute about it. If you're not sure you're okay with it, just sit back for a bit, and listen with your heart. Something will happen.

Six months later, a situation presented itself that I thought was a proper way to honor him. I was glad for those earlier decisions. This memorial was closer to where I lived, and if I wanted, I could go there and see it. There may be options that you will not find out about until later. When those types of things happen, I take them as signs that things worked out as they should have. I have found those options will come from unexpected events, people, or places you didn't know even existed.

Are there relatives who don't agree with what I did for either of my parents? Possibly. But remember, we're not responsible for how they feel. Try not to be too hard on yourself. We did what we could with the limited help and support before, during, and especially after our parents died. That's all that matters.

CHAPTER 11
MORE STUFF?

What do I do with this? Some things will leave you scratching your head in wonder. Others will amaze and/or disgust you. But I'm betting if you examine your stuff, you'll see similarities. From my experiences of going through everything at both of my parents' houses, I realize we all own way too much stuff. But as I sorted through their belongings, I realized these belongings, and our attachment to them, means the most to the person they belong to. Their attraction to the item may not be apparent to someone else. But again, I challenge you to investigate your belongings, and you'll see a similar pattern; I know I did.

You'll find that you keep a lot of their things and toss a substantial number of things with little or no value into the regular garbage. You can take bulky items to a landfill. They charge a fee based on the weight of the items you're dumping. You'll throw many things away, depending on how long your parents lived in their home, the size of the house, and outdoor spaces like garages and sheds.

What do you do with this stuff that you have inherited as your stuff now, your responsibility? You have several options.

Thrift Stores

Most cities and even smaller towns have local Goodwill Donation Stores or other thrift stores. They will be happy to take all you have if it is in good condition. Keep an itemized list of these items and get a receipt from the thrift store or charity so you can deduct the items on your parent's final tax return. You can deliver the items to their facility or find out if they provide a pickup service. It'll vary by city and location. I contacted my local store, went over the items I had for donation, and scheduled a pickup with them. You may be able to arrange this too, if you sizable items and don't have a way to transport them.

I donated some items to the Big Brother Big Sister charity, since my mom had regularly donated to them. I never asked why she preferred that charity. The story I told myself was she'd been close to her older brother, and it made her think of him. It was one of those oddball questions that come up after they die that you didn't know to ask them about when they were alive.

Estate Sales, Auction Houses, and Rental Spaces

If I had known more about Estate Sales, what they were, and how they worked, I would've chosen this option for my mom's belongings. You'll want to make this decision early on, before you've given away, or hauled away, or thrown away anything. Estate sales take place because of someone's death, a divorce, foreclosure, or relocation. If you own quality or antique items, the estate-sale option may be an exceptional opportunity. You can have estate sales for other reasons besides a death. The most common are retirement, downsizing, job relocation, divorce, or bankruptcy.

I thought people just roamed through your home at leisure, but it doesn't work like that. A professional estate-sale agent will come to your home, appraise your items, and schedule your sale. You will need to have enough sale items to draw a sizeable crowd. The company will require you to meet their minimum total value for your sale (the company I researched was $3,000). They may schedule it for one day or more, depending on the number of items.

The estate-sale company receives anywhere between 25% to 50% from the sale. But they organize everything, so it is worth what they charge, and you get help with the entire event. First, they come and set up everything; then they price it and sell it. When it's over, they even clean up! They may also decide to buy the items which didn't sell for a reduced rate. If you choose the right company, this process could be one of your best decisions.

They compile their own list of people whom they invite to their sales, and only a small group of people come into the home at a time. They may contact specific dealers with a particular interest in certain items. For example, let's suppose you inherited a Hawaiian art collection. A dealer specializing in Hawaiian art will pay more for those items than someone who's planning to resell to another dealer or a flea market customer.

Companies offering Estate Sale Buyouts are also available. They make an offer for the entire estate, and they will pay you in one lump sum. For this option, the sale is complete once you have accepted their offer. Then they come pick up all the items and take them to their own location to process and sell.

The antique items are the ones you may agonize over the most. With antiques, you'll need to either hire someone or do research on your own. If you conduct your own research, I recommend purchasing access to a reputable database to get prices. The same tools may facilitate finding buyers as well. These have the potential to be worth quite a bit of money. If you like the item and have room, you can keep it. If you keep them, insure them through your home or renter's insurance. Then add them to your will and designate who you want to leave them to upon your death.

You can rent booths at antique or auction houses, and the company, or an auctioneer, will sell your items. This is an excellent way to get your items in front of more prospective buyers. In most places, the fees will cover insurance on your items, credit-card transaction fees, and collecting and submitting the sales taxes to the state or county. Search online for locations in your area.

Property to Sell

Keep the house? Sell the house? Rent it out? How do you do that? What if you already have a home or a place to live? Do you want to live where it's located? This will probably be the most significant monetary item you'll deal with after your parent(s) die.

Houses are tricky because their value will rely on the rise and fall of the housing market. It'll depend on location, neighborhood, size of the home, and any extras like a pool or room for an RV in the backyard. When my mom bought her house in the late '80s, it was in a friendly middle class, mixed ethnic neighborhood. By the mid-2010s, it had made national news as the scene of a serial killer's latest rage. His most recent victim lived three doors down from my mom. That was too close for my comfort.

Most of the time she lived in that neighborhood, I had lived in another state. She had drifted along with the community and its changes for more than 30 years. She was nearing 80 years old and loved her house, and she hadn't thought she should or could move. Then I came along and asked, "Why not?" All it takes is time, effort, and money, and you can do whatever fits your budget.

If you keep the property and rent it out, do some research on rentals in the city and county where the property is located. You may need to hire a rental agent or management company to facilitate the rental for you. I suggest talking with someone who rents their property in your area. Find out what types of issues they encounter and whether you can make a decent return on your investment versus selling the property.

When my dad died, I inherited a mobile home. A 35-year-old mobile home that had fallen into disrepair because his health hadn't allowed him to keep up with it. I didn't want the mobile home, and it would take a lot of cleaning and repair to the flooring to make it safe and livable. I had no family or friends who lived nearby. My aunts and uncles, my dad's siblings, had lived in the same mobile home park but had died many years earlier.

Early on, I had lived in my dad's home, too, and also across the street from him. I didn't see him every day, but we could see each other's front doors. He'd been the only reason I had stayed there before my big move eight years earlier. Now there was no one. If he didn't live there, then there was no need for me to be somewhere I didn't want to be.

In both situations involving my parent's homes, I decided to sell, give away, reuse, repurpose what I could, and throw away the items too personal to give away. There ended up being a lot of those, more than I thought. It was an odd thing. I just didn't want someone else to have them. If you have lost a parent, you may have had similar feelings. I didn't want to keep some of the items, but I also didn't want anyone else to get them.

Selling Items Online

You can sell your items using online venues and apps. This option will depend upon your comfort level, time commitment, and patience to deal with the apps, returns, and customer complaints (theirs and yours). Take a quality photo of the item, write a detailed description, and post the article. In some apps, you can take online payments and then arrange to meet them somewhere in person or ship it to them. Get a neighbor to come over when you sell to someone in person if you're on your own like me. I had a pleasant experience and sold several pieces of small furniture. I could get more for them that way than selling them at a traditional garage sale.

These are a few of the standard venues available: eBay, Craigslist, Facebook, and Etsy. Some venues specialize in specific categories or products, such as clothing, vintage items, furniture, electronics, or media such as CDs, DVDs, Games, and Books (both print and digital). These are just a few examples of the specific categories that are available. Your usage will depend on your comfort level and ability with websites and apps.

Using online venues and apps to sell your items involves a time factor. Most of them charge a fee or take a commission percentage on the items sold. Each one is a bit different. Read their rules and fee schedules for more information. Read the online reviews on the apps and make sure they're reputable companies before using them. New apps and venues become available all the time.

CHAPTER 12
WILL SOMEONE ACTUALLY BUY THIS STUFF?

I found a stack of 78-LP records in my mom's closet. I assumed they came out of an old jukebox since they didn't have any protective covers, and they had severe scratches. The titles were from the '40s and '50s. You'll stare at these and wonder what to do with them and if they're worth anything. And let's not forget the two big boxes of 8-track tapes! They don't even make players for those anymore.

You'll assess stuff like this and debate with yourself, "Well, there's someone who wants to buy these, right?" Or you may conclude, "These are old and in terrible shape, oh the heck with it, I'm just going to put them in the trash, bye — done — gone!" This is one of those tasks you'll try to second-guess yourself but don't.

All the research, posting, and selling takes time, and you may spend that time and still not get a sale. Remember, your time is valuable. But if you have time and think you'll enjoy the task, it may be a desirable choice. Research the items and make sure they aren't online offered for free, which would nullify your sale. Remember, with all this, you have choices, you have options. You can sell them, store them, or toss them.

My parents had owned more than 200 vinyl albums, and I was sure they hadn't played them in decades. Most of them were easy listening music from the 1940's and 1950's, with a couple Creedence Clearwater Revival albums from the 1960's in the mix. I created a spreadsheet, found a few specialty buyers online, contacted them, and emailed them the list. I found out these albums were so old that most of the recordings were available for free online or weren't something people were buying. In fact, I couldn't even give them away to the buyers.

To Store or Not to Store

You may need to rent a storage space if you have many items to sell and don't have room to store things where you live. I rented one to keep my mom's things, which I intended to sell. Be diligent if you decide that you're going to rent space at a storage facility. It can quickly go from something you only intended to rent for six months, and the next thing you know, it's two years later. If you won't use it or don't sell it, paying for storage devalues the items every month you make that payment.

Having items in a storage unit is something I've tried to avoid. My dad had a storage unit that he rented for more than 20 years. My guess was he never even saw the stuff after he put it in there. After 20 years, he didn't even remember what was there, only that he hadn't needed it for 20 years! A few years before he died, he said he paid some people to clean it out and take the items. He hadn't even bothered to go see what was there. He wouldn't recoup the money he had spent on the storage, so he rationalized why bother with it at that point.

Not Like on TV

I've learned so many things because of research I've had to do related to my parent(s) deaths. Matters that I thought I knew.

One of the interesting facts that I learned along the way is that safe-deposit boxes at the bank aren't for what most of us presumed. Let me see a show of hands for how many people thought rich people kept their jewelry and cash stashed in a safe deposit box at their favorite bank. Yep, me too! But they don't. In fact, the bank advises against it.

The bank doesn't provide insurance on the contents because they don't know what's in the box. However, you can tell your insurance company what's in the box, and they can insure them under your mortgage or renter's insurance policies. I had never had a safe deposit box, and silly me thought it was for jewels and cash like what you see in the movies. Nope, it's used to store copies of important papers or backups of computer files, at least that's what the associates at the bank told me.

When you add to or remove items, you go with a bank employee into the vault, retrieve your box, and then go by yourself into a secluded room. When you finish adding or removing something from the box, the bank employee goes with you, and you put the box back into the vault. The only protection the bank provides is the storing of your items in their key access vault.

The rules about the box can vary from bank to bank. They give you two keys. There are also specific regulations concerning access to it after you die and the access allowed for the person to whom you have given the key. Keep in mind, you only have access to the box during the hours on the days that the bank is open. If the bank must close for an extended period, you will not have access to it.

Your Time is Valuable

Once I cleared out my dad's personal things from the mobile home, I sold it with most of the furniture still in it, along with the contents of a backyard shed. If you're dealing with something like this, examine the sum of it all. It's best to make it part of a package deal unless you need to spend a little sentimental time with it. Did I give away a lot as part of that deal?

Yes, I did. I knew I did. But I also realized there was a myriad of tools, thousands of nuts, bolts, screws, and nails, and that going through them wouldn't be an effective use of my time.

I know there may have been treasures hidden underneath all that stuff. But it was another one of those times where I had to just walk away, not glance back, and be okay with it later. By selling those items with the home, it allowed me to complete the task sooner. Then it was time for me to leave, drive back across the country and try to piece "my life" back together.

My mom and I had discussed moving her to a new home several months before she died. Because of those discussions, she started sorting through her belongings, boxing up what she wanted to keep, and donating what she didn't want to keep. There also were a few items she asked if I was interested in them or if I cared if she gave it to someone else. It surprised me she had asked me, and in fact, I thought it was odd that she asked me.

Remember that people can change, their perspectives can shift, even our own. Embrace those shifts, but don't spend too much time in your head questioning them. Don't spend too much time in your head thinking about whether there was a shift, either. Do contemplate doing what's best for you before, during, and after their deaths. Be available for as many meaningful conversations with your parent(s) as possible.

It turned out to be helpful that my mom had been in the planning stages of moving. It had given her the chance to inspect her own belongings and decide what she wanted to keep, give away, or plan to give away. This was one of those shifts she had experienced. Here we were, two adults discussing the items she owned and their future after her death. Those conversations held a lot of emotional value for both of us. After her death, I realized we could have had more of those conversations. It was important to me to identify where something had come from, and who owned it before. Sometimes I needed the answer to "What's this?"

That's why I mention it, especially for an only-child. It won't be easy, but you'll be glad you took the time to partake in those conversations with them and learn the stories about the belongings that filled their lives. If you don't know that information, you will hope to find a note or a photo to help you identify it. Otherwise, you'll throw something away because, without that story, it's just another item to sit on the shelf, stuff into a box, or give away.

CHAPTER 13

JUST A FEW MORE THINGS

Depending on how close you were to your parent(s), this may be the first time you've even seen their personal belongings. You may have never been in their dressers or closets. Regardless, prepare yourself. There may be things you've never seen before. Expect there will be many odds and ends, a few really bizarre odds, and several sorts of ends to clear out if they've lived at their residence for 20-plus years.

One of the more challenging aspects is you'll go through those items on your own. Many nights I spent unpacking boxes that had things packed in them for years. Sometimes it's interesting to read the old newspapers used to wrap around the items and view the advertisements from an earlier time. Finding other things you enjoy will help you through the process. There were many items I wondered what to do with. The kitchen items were a little comical. I mean, truly, "How many sets of measuring cups and spoons does someone need? And my goodness, wow, you still had this? I remember that from when I was five years old!"

My dad had a spare room, and it had become the catch-all room. He had boxes and boxes of receipts, unbroken parts from appliances like coffeepot carafes without their coffeemakers, spare computer parts, or old printers where something quit working but still had other functional components, etc. But I catch myself keeping the same things. I come by it honestly enough, though; both my parents were that way! They owned or hoarded things, depending on your perspective, just in case they needed it later.

So, let's see "How many pairs of pliers does one person need?" Well, I have four different ones of my own, and he had six, and goodness she had, yes, eleven pairs of pliers. They were even assorted sizes too, like small, medium, large, and one extra-extra-small. Now I know where I got the trait from! "But I don't need 21 pairs of pliers, just these three, and yes, I'll keep this one too." There will be situations that will leave you laughing and shaking your head. And others will help you know yourself better as well.

I try to put in perspective the era in which they grew up. Years filled with several wars, a Great Depression, and the assassination of leaders, senators, and presidents. Tumultuous and different from the years I grew up in. It's hard to picture our parents as children, and it's easy to forget they were once children, too. What was your view of your parents? Did you see them how they were, or did it seem as though they were characters in a movie or a play? Often, I saw them as my critics when, in fact, they were my silent cheerleaders.

The Stuff You Actually Should Keep

These are those specific items that embodied who my parents were. Please, please, keep those items that your senses will always associate with them. You'll wish you had, and it's usually only a few items. Do you know of items belonging to your parents that embody them? These are the things you can see, smell, taste, or hear. They are so familiar to your subconscious and a part of who you are. It reminds you of them through your senses.

Find those types of things, things unique to whom they were to you. Gather them and keep them for yourself. You'll know them when you see them or smell them, and it's okay to keep them. Take a little time to get to know them in a sensory way before you give them away.

One of the more challenging aspects will be to not feel guilty or selfish. Don't buy into our stereotype. This isn't beneficial for your soul. Remember, these are the only two people who you'll ever feel this close to unless you have children of your own. Don't bury your feelings about something to spare someone else's thoughts or feelings about you. You've been doing that your whole life, and it's time for it to change.

His Stuff

You know when something hangs or sits in the same place for a long time, and after a while, you don't "see" it anymore? For as long as I could remember, my dad's firefighting helmet hung on the wall in his mobile home. It had always hung in the same place. Although I didn't recall him telling me any stories about it, I knew it was his fire helmet, and I thought a little more about it.

I had never taken it off the wall, held it in my hands, or seen the inside. Inside the helmet, my dad had written the fire station's number and the years he'd worked at each one. I could feel my dad's presence in that helmet. Smelled the smoke on it. It smelled like him. The little girl in me remembered the same smell from the mornings when I was growing up. It signified he was home from working overnight, or sometimes several days at the fire station. I remembered the familiar scent. It was his scent, his cologne, so to speak, and I couldn't part with it.

Her Stuff

I don't remember being aware of my mom's perfume though it was a scent she wore every day of my life. A few days after she'd died, I was in her bathroom, and I picked up the bottle.

I didn't even know the name of the perfume. The bottle had been in the same spot on her dresser for so long, I didn't "see" it anymore. But when I took the cap off and smelled it, I didn't have to see it to know it was the smell I always associated with her. It was just like when I picked up the fire helmet and smelled the smoke on it. My subconscious was familiar with that smell.

One day my best friend was with me in my mom's truck, and she started sneezing. She was the one who told me the truck smelled like my mom. I had never noticed it, but she was right. It did! It took a few weeks before I realized the clothes in her closet had her perfume on them too, and every time I opened her closet door, I experienced her. It made me think of all those times she'd met me at the front door when I came over to her house. Of course, she'd been wearing it, but again I had never been aware of it on a conscious level. I ordered a fresh bottle of the perfume, and I wear it when I go out, and I also sprayed a bit in the closet on my clothes.

People Will Ask for Things

People will make requests for items. They may approach you themselves, or ask through someone else, if they had a relationship with your parent but not with you. When someone asks for a memento or an object that belonged to one of your parents, it may be best to wait to give them an answer. Remember, you don't have to give up anything; this is your choice, and you don't have to feel bad about your decision. It's not an acceptable or unacceptable thing. It has nothing to do with whether you value the person, either. You may not even know the person.

My cousin had told me he would like to have my dad's firefighting helmet. This was the same cousin who visited after my dad died. The same one who had called and told me I needed to figure out a way to get to South Carolina to take care of my dad because he needed to get back to his home. The same cousin who I had never met before and hadn't known even existed. Before I had time to think about it, I told him I would give him the helmet. And it was what I planned to do until the day I took it down off the wall.

It was hard to tell my cousin I had changed my mind. I didn't decide to hurt him on purpose, but I hadn't been aware of how much that one object epitomized who my dad was in a way no other memento could. The helmet had been part of the gear my dad received when he started his firefighting career in the mid-1950's. It was with him throughout the entirety of his 25-year career. The fire helmet doesn't hang on my wall in a prominent place. It's in the closet in a box, and I'm okay with it. I know it's there. Maybe someday I'll part with it, but not today.

There was a request from a friend of my mom's for an item that I couldn't honor. The item was a beautiful green velvet-like blouse which she'd sewn herself. Green was my mom's favorite color. She had loved that blouse, and I couldn't part with it. It hangs in my closet now, and I have never worn it because it doesn't fit me. Do I feel selfish? Yes, a little, but it's okay.

CHAPTER 14

YES, THERE'S MORE STUFF

I kept more of my mom's things than my dad's. Perhaps it was because he died before her, so I had the other experience as a comparison. Or, like me, you may have to factor in the cost of transporting them to another location thousands of miles away or storing them if you don't have a plan for your next move. The relationships with your parent(s) before their death will have less to do with what you keep than you think it will.

Another essential task to complete before they die is to ask to view any collections they own. Ask them questions about them. For me, these collections have been the most time-consuming and challenging items my parents owned. Poke around if you aren't aware of or don't find any out on display. If they have them, you need to discuss what to do with them after they die.

Each of my parents owned a collection, which was more than your amateur fare. I had seen most of what was in my mom's collection. My dad's collection was more of a mystery because it had been in storage, and I didn't get to see it until after he died. There were a couple smaller collections that were a little more challenging but were manageable.

Neither of them told me much relating to their collections. Nor offered suggestions for what I should do with them after they died. Investigate options for managing the collection if you don't want to sort and catalog it. You will need to inquire which companies can appraise it and their processes for payment. There may also be local resources that can review the collection too. It can be a little tricky to find reliable sources, so be thorough in your research.

Her Collection

My mom was the steward of a sports-card collection that belonged to her significant other. She'd spent many hours organizing the cards after his death, and it helped her heal a little of her grief. She took what had been a mess of cards thrown into cardboard boxes and put them in protective plastic sleeves inside binders. The collection comprised over 50 binders that she had shelved on a bookcase in the closet. After she finished organizing them, she advertised them and got a few offers. She declined those offers because they weren't willing to buy them all. All 27,000 of them! They were only interested in purchasing the valuable cards, and she wouldn't sell those by themselves.

Cards, cards, and more cards! I gathered information from the baseball, football, basketball, hockey cards, and other sports memorabilia and put it into spreadsheets. I paid fees to access databases to look up what they were worth. It was like I enrolled in a course on sports memorabilia and all the intricacies of collecting it, and I don't even like sports! They had scales and specific attributes that also played a role in deciding the price for a card. That included things such as the year(s) the player played, the card's condition, if they honored the player, or held a record, affected the card's price.

It would take a lot of time to sort through the multiples, different versions, and conditions. I found out that in the 1980's, they had mass-produced thousands of baseball cards and that they were worth little to nothing to a collector. Only a few cards will garner a decent sum because they're rare or old. After you find those cards, then you must track down a willing buyer. Sites like eBay were excellent resources, but because several cards show so many listings available, it was hard to pin down an exact price.

In this example of the sports cards, you must ask yourself if it would be worth the time to go through all these cards to find the proverbial needle in the haystack. If you end with 100, or 200 cards out of 27,000 that are worth something, that's a lot of cards to go through to find just a couple hundred. This could be a genuine challenge to weigh the worth of the cards versus your time.

His Collection

I had heard snippets about my dad's coin collection over the years, but I had never seen it. I had seen a few books with wheat pennies and Mercury dimes over the years, and I remembered seeing some Kennedy half dollars. I thought the collection comprised a few coin books. He also owned the requisite state quarter collection that every over 50-year-old coin collector had bought. Each of these quarters came in its own plastic protective case. A bit of research showed those coins were still worth only twenty-five cents apiece, even as uncirculated coins.

When I received the collection, I found out it was more than a few coin books. There were rolls of assorted coins. Some were old, some were silver, and some were newer. There were some foreign coins and collectors' coins sealed in plastic. First, I needed to figure out what was in the collection. So, I started creating an inventory spreadsheet like I did with the cards. Then using my "amateur learn as you go method," I started figuring out their value.

If he had an inventory, I couldn't find any spreadsheets or logs to tell me that information. I had nothing that told me how much they were worth together or individually, and their worth varies because the prices of silver and gold fluctuate daily. Many silver coins are worth more than the currency's actual denomination because of their silver content, unless it's a rarity. If you spend time researching and paying for database access, you may find you possess one of those rare coins, and then again, you may not.

I still wonder why he said nothing to me about the collection. Had he looked for the ones that were rare or had imperfections and were worth more? What did he intend I do with these? Was I to keep them? Sell them? How was I going to figure out how much they were worth? And how much time was this going to take? I have so many questions to ask him. If only I could! We could have spent those hours when we waited in the ER for them to admit him to the hospital discussing things like this. It would have been the perfect time. At least I can say I'm more interested in the coins as a collectible item than the sports cards.

More Collections

There was another collection that I found when cleaning out my mom's house. She collected matchbooks back in the 1960's and 1970's. There were at least 200 books, and I'm sure I'm underestimating the exact amount. Think of it, there's a small canvas suitcase, circa Avon 1970's, and inside are these matchbooks. At first, you think, "Hey, cool, I remember this collection from a long time ago. Wow, I didn't know she still had these!" Then the realization hits you, "Wow, major fire hazard! And, really! Who's going to want these smelly old sulfur matchbooks?" Nostalgia creeps back in, and you look at them, "But oh, check out this one, that's cool!" Then that practical voice raises its head and exclaims, "Hello, fire hazard, significant fire hazard! These need to be outside, like now! But what if it catches fires in the trash can? Well, it's not in the house! Okay, okay."

Two months later, you're on eBay, and you notice some matchbooks similar to the ones you threw away. A few are selling at a higher price than you would've thought someone would pay for an old matchbook. You'll remember tossing those matchbooks and catch yourself ruminating, "Yep, I should've kept them and sold them." But let's not forget common sense in this scenario. "Old matchbooks, lots of them. Fire hazard!!" That my dad was a firefighter no doubt played into my decision that the best thing was to get rid of them, and of utmost importance was to get them out of the house! Further research about how to ship flammable objects nipped this rumination in the bud. Sometimes you just need a little more information to confirm you made the right decision!

My dad also owned another collection. This collection included a large cabinet that held all his rifles, shotguns, pistols, and ammunition. He had always told me he planned to give that collection to one of his brother's sons, my cousin. Thankfully before he ended up in the hospital, he had contacted my cousin, and he came and got them. Obviously, my dad had no way of knowing that he would go into the hospital a few months later and never return home. I don't care for guns, but both my parents were at ease using and owning them.

A Comfort I Never Shared

I think my uneasiness with guns started when I was four or five years old. I remember hearing the telling (and multiple retellings) of the story of what happened at our house early one winter morning. It goes something like this....

The story starts with a recap of my dad's annual hunting trip to Wyoming with his friend Stewart. They hauled butt all night across four states, and he had just gotten home and got all his gear and stuff unloaded from the van. They had a rewarding trip. "We didn't see very many deer this year, but we saw a lot of elk. There must have been at least fifteen in this one herd... blah, blah, blah."

My dad had lots of experience with guns and handled them for many years for hunting and personal use. It was still early in the morning, and my mom and I were still sleeping, so he figured he would clean his rifle before we got up. He laid out all the cleaning supplies on the kitchen table, brought the scope up to his eye, squinted, aimed at a tile right above the stove in the kitchen, and pulled the trigger.

Well, the rifle went off, and a bullet blasted through the tile in the kitchen's corner wall, traveled twelve feet down the hallway, curved a little, and entered my bedroom. The bullet traveled in a diagonal direction across my bedroom for another twelve feet and lodged in the wall right above my small blue chair. If it had been during the day, chances are that I could've been sitting in that chair.

To this day, I still see a detailed movie-like version of the scene, with different angles of the scene's action. But I've no recollection of the actual event. My movie version developed from hearing my parents re-tell the story multiple times to other people. I remember that you could see into the kitchen from the hallway. Later, you could always see where they patched and filled in the hole in the wall. As an only-child, I overheard many stories that I wouldn't have heard if I had spent less time around the adults and were more pre-occupied with goofing off with siblings.

My ex-husband took me to a gun range several times, hoping to improve my comfort level about guns. I would aim the pistol at the target, squeeze my eyes shut, squeeze the trigger, and hope to hit the target. I told him that if I ever hit anything with a bullet, it would be because of divine intervention or blind luck! This was one thing I had no interest in, and I still don't care about them or want to own one. I don't care if others own them. I just have no need for one myself.

. . . Until the day I was going through my mom's sock drawer after she died. I hadn't thought about guns or collections of firearms. Then I found not just one, not two, but three personal guns! What was I supposed to do with these? With no intimate knowledge or backstory about them, I was at a loss, and she was the only one who had that information.

I'll stress again that these are the reasons to have those conversations and find out about the things you may not even realize your parent(s) own. Discover the items that you would feel uncomfortable dealing with that you think they own. Ask them questions. Look around at everything in their homes and yards. Ask them lots of questions.

CHAPTER 15
WHAT I KNEW ABOUT DEATH AND DYING

Don't feel stupid if you know nothing about death and dying and what you should do. It's more common than you might think. Most of what I had gathered about it, I had pieced together from conversations I overheard from relatives. The other pieces came from what I had seen on television shows and movies. Again, I wouldn't rely on those as reliable sources of information. I would need to learn and figure out most of it as I went, and most of what I found wasn't useful. Yes, information is available on the internet, but you must sort and sift through it, decipher the information that overlaps and contradicts, and ensure that the source is reliable.

I want this death and dying event to be better for you, the adult only-child. It's the focal point of this book and the primary reason I wrote it. I want to help ease the discomfort that comes from not having any idea what to do. If there's no family left to help, you may feel more alone than you ever have in your entire life. You'll have to decide a lot of things, and these decisions won't be straightforward, either. There will be times you will need to bend and curve and stand firm to get through this. A lot of decisions will feel overwhelming if you're required to make them for your parent(s).

Always make sure you're listening to the voice that guides you. You need to listen to it more than the people around you because they'll be dealing with their own struggles. If they're not an only-child, they'll perceive even less about what you're going through emotionally, mentally, and spiritually. They'll comprehend even less if they've not experienced the loss of a parent.

I Didn't Understand

One thing that sucks about getting older is that more people you know, along with your own family, die. As an adult only-child, you may be like me and learn about this life event through trial and error. Nobody had shared that information with me. Because my family circle was so small, I hadn't heard many stories about death from others. There were no siblings with an extended family to listen to their stories. There was no significant other, so I could listen to their family stories. Without children, there was no connection to other families with children to hear of their stories.

There were no experiences to help me know how lost someone felt, especially when a parent died, and that it differs from when other family members die. I hadn't understood the grief someone feels who has lost a parent. Is this the case with most people? Yes, I think it is. Before I had to face those realities, I wish that someone would have talked to me about these things.

I'll give them the benefit of the doubt because I couldn't conceive how I would feel or experience my parent's death. It may have never crossed their mind that I didn't know any specifics, that I would deal with their deaths by myself, and it would overwhelm me. The challenge for an adult only-child is to get and also ask for help. More often than not, we've been self-sufficient in so many areas of our lives and are more comfortable being by ourselves than with other people. Most of the people I've known have siblings, children, significant others, or all of the above. They're not alone.

The Other Funerals

My father's parents died many years before I was born, so I only knew them from photos. My father was the oldest of four siblings. There was one photo of his dad, a large black-and-white image with my dad standing on his dad's lap. They were both smiling. Something rare for my dad.

His father was not around when his mom died, and he was the one who had to make those tough decisions. He was only 17. This was in the early 1950's, and I don't know if he had help or not. They had little money, so there weren't as many options available. I would like to think his aunts or uncles helped him with the decisions. Dealing with that loss at such an early age couldn't have been easy. He also had three younger siblings to take care of, and the youngest sibling ended up going to a foster home.

My father's three siblings had traditional funerals with caskets, viewings, and burials. I didn't know what transpired during the plan for those funerals. I didn't perceive whether there were previous plans or the process for the dispersal of their personal property and belongings. Both brothers had served more than 25 years in the military, so I figured plans were in place because of their years of service. The only thing I remember about the funerals I attended was how uncomfortable I was and that I didn't have anyone to talk to about my feelings.

My dad's sister and her husband lived in the same mobile-home park where my dad lived. She died of a heart attack two months after I got married, and like the old cliché you hear about it, she was there one moment and gone the next. One of my dad's brothers also lived in the same mobile-home park. Six years after his sister died, his brother was admitted into the hospital because of diabetic complications. He was there for two weeks, and then he died. My dad's other brother, who lived in another state, died from diabetes and lung-cancer complications three years before my dad died.

Although my mom had two older siblings, she'd been the one responsible for the funerals of her mother, father, and brother. Her father lived with us when I was 10 years old. They hospitalized him because of complications from atherosclerosis, which most people interpret as hardening of the arteries. They amputated one of his legs, and then not long after, they removed his other leg. I would go with my mom to the hospital. I remember sometimes being there for hours. There was a large lobby you entered on the ground floor, and I would wait there while she went up to his room. One time I was in that lobby for so long, I thought she may have left and forgotten me there. He died four days before my 11th birthday.

I don't remember being at his funeral, only that it took place in Nebraska. Nor do I remember anyone talking to me about it. I had no idea how you should act or what you should do when someone died. My mother must've flown there or ridden with other family members because I accompanied my dad on an overnight straight-through drive from Missouri to Nebraska. He must have only had one 8-track tape with us because all I remember hearing was the Everly Brothers playing over and over all night. My mom's mother and brother died during the years when I had sparse contact with her. So, I hadn't taken part in any planning, nor did I attend their funerals.

The last funeral I attended was for my dad's brother in 2001, and I never plan to go to another one. I refuse to put myself through a process that, for me, is traumatic, unpleasant, and morbid. When I was going through photos that belonged to my parents, I would see photos from someone's funeral. There were always photos of the deceased lying in their casket. To me, that was the most morbid thing you could do at a funeral other than viewing the dead body of the person. It didn't scare me, it just creeped me out, and I could never figure out why they thought it was imperative to take that photo.

My mom had donated her body, and starting with my phone call to the donation company the night she died, they managed the entire cremation process. There were two reasons I thought the process was noteworthy. I received a notice in my mailbox to pick up a package at the post office, and until the mail person offered me condolences as he handed me my box, I did not know I was going to receive her ashes via USPS Priority Mail. Well, hello, Mom!! The second was that the job I had resigned after my mom died was with the USPS. But I must have missed the section covering shipments of someone's ashes to their loved ones during my training. I had no idea they did that, and I wondered if my mom had gotten the special "Fragile sticker" box treatment during her USPS journey!

Care for the Dying

My parents were like night and day with their medical care. My mom had a list of doctors and specialists that she visited every month, two months, six months, or every year at the same time. She had a daily schedule for her medications and took them like clockwork. My dad had not seen the inside of a regular doctor's office for at least eight years, and he did not take any medications.

My dad ended up in a hospital because he fell and lost his ability to walk. After all the standard imaging tests, the doctors recommended surgery on the vertebrae in his lower back. Because I was familiar with my dad's history and have had a few surgeries myself, I told him I wasn't sure surgery was a promising idea. But the surgeon convinced him he could fix his back and get him walking again. My dad opted to have major surgery on his lower back at the age of 82, and the surgery would take place right before I started my cross-country move.

Within a few weeks of his surgery, the doctors diagnosed him with lymphoma. He opted to receive radiation treatments for the large, growing lump on his upper shoulder. Again, I told him I wasn't sure it was a promising idea, and those treatments were never successful. The doctors at the hospital then transferred him to a rehabilitation facility to receive an intensive form of physical therapy to regain his mobility. My dad never did regain the use of his legs.

They assigned him a caseworker at the rehabilitation facility whose focus was to ensure the insurance payments to cover his stay. Most health insurance covers only a certain number of days at those facilities or may not cover it at all. They will also want to make sure of your plan for where your parent will go after leaving the rehabilitation facility.

For almost three months, my dad went back and forth from the hospital to the rehabilitation facility every couple of weeks. During his rehabilitation stays, he would start having problems breathing, leading to pneumonia, accompanied by a fever. This would prompt transport to the hospital's emergency room and admission back into the hospital. Each time they readmitted him to the hospital, he got a little bit worse than the previous transfer. It was as if he were climbing a staircase. He would go one step up, then two or three steps down, then up one, then back down two.

Throughout that time, I was trying to figure out where he would go if they released him from the rehabilitation facility. Because he was a veteran, he could go to a Veterans' Nursing Home. Check online for those facility locations. A person can only move to a veteran's home in the state where they've been living. I was filling out paperwork and talking with the administrators about his admittance there, but he was on a waiting list, a lengthy list. They would only move him up on that waiting list if there was a dramatic change in his health, which met their criteria for that move. I didn't know from week to week where he was going to go upon his release. My biggest concern was that he was running out of covered days at the rehabilitation facility.

You can research placing someone in a nursing home or assisted-living facility. This is another one of those areas that may not be as straightforward as you think unless you have previous experience and knowledge of how this works. First off, health insurance doesn't cover these. Social Security and/ or pension payments will transfer to the nursing facility to cover their stay. Your parent may have a small amount left over that they can use for personal items, or they may not. You may have to provide more funds to cover the facility's entire cost through a savings account. You would have to sign this account over to the facility, too.

Hospice care can be beneficial if you're the sole caretaker. Again, this was one of those things I thought I knew a little about, but I didn't. There are rules concerning hospice care and when it becomes available for your parent. First, hospice care isn't available until the doctor treating your parent makes a diagnosis stating that the patient has an illness or disease that's terminal. Upon that diagnosis, the patient and/or family decide whether to continue or forgo any treatments, medications, surgeries that the hospital can provide to the patient.

It's imperative to keep in mind that once you've declined the services available for the patient at the hospital, you'll need to move them to another location. Hospitals or rehab facilities don't administer hospice care. In this case, the patient, or parent, moves to the patient's home or a family member's home. My dad's house wasn't livable, especially not for someone in his state of health. In fact, I was clearing 30-years of stuff from that home, hoping to sell it to someone willing to invest in repairing and fixing up a 35-year-old mobile home to make it livable.

CHAPTER 16
LAST RESPECTS

When my dad died, there were no step-by-step instructions left to tell me what he wanted, so I made it up as I went along. Going through photos that belonged to my dad, several of which I had never seen, prompted my creativity to create a memory book using those photos. I filled the pages with the significant people and events from his life. I used the pins from his formal Fire Department uniform to secure the pages together into an album. I also created a memorial card highlighting the momentous events in his life, accompanied by a picture of him in his Fire Department uniform. It all came together, precisely right, and I created albums for each of my cousins, my dad's brother's children. This felt like a respectful and proper way to honor his life since there wouldn't be a traditional funeral.

When my mom died, there were no step-by-step instructions left to tell me what she wanted, so I also made it up as I went along. She had collected seeds from her hollyhocks for years. She was so proud of the ones she grew in her yard, most of which grew taller than she was! I planned to get small envelopes for the seeds and include them with a memorial card that I could send out. She loved these flowers, and they had given her many hours of joy. I thought it would be a way to share a part of her with others.

When You're Not Up to the Task

The Christmas after my mom died, she received 27 Christmas cards, but I only recognized three of the senders. I struggled over her death and the realizations that came with it, which became overwhelming when coupled with my dad's death only two years prior. The memorial card with the hollyhock seeds never quite came together over the summer. I realized I was putting a lot of pressure on myself to send something to people I didn't even know. By this time, her ashes were already in South Dakota. The people there knew she had died. Any other friends, the ones I knew, I had contacted not long after she died.

Have you ever thought you needed to do something as a memorial for one or both of your parents, but it didn't happen, or you weren't able to pull it together? Did you make connections with family or talk to them about the family you heard about, but didn't know? Do you have a family tree or genealogy of your family? Have you ever thought about finding a secret family?

I don't have instantaneous connections to distant or unknown relatives. I'm not "instant" like that, and I doubt if it will ever change for me. Whatever secrets died with my mom or dad I would prefer to keep that way. It won't serve or improve my life, and sometimes things are just what they are. Remember, you're the only one who must be okay with your decisions.

You've just experienced the most significant responsibility of your life. The arrangements and obligations to care for your parents were the most challenging decisions you ever had to make. Anyone who second guesses or questions your choices is disrespectful, and you don't have to be okay with that. People with those viewpoints aren't aware of the effects this event has had on your life. They don't have a clue that without your parents, the whole state of your world has changed.

It All Works Out Later

I returned to my mom's house to figure out where my life would go next after my dad died. I shipped all my belongings across the country and stored them in her garage. I didn't know where I was going or what I would do for work, and it would be two years before my world was upright and stable again.

After receiving my dad's military service flag from the funeral home, I bought a nice cherry-wood edged glass display case to put it in. I thought it was the thing to do, even though I didn't have a house or a mantel, with or without a fireplace, to display it. My mom had her brother's military service flag in a case but also didn't have a place to display it at her house. His ashes are in a small crypt surrounded by hundreds of others at the military cemetery near her.

One day we drove to the cemetery to discuss options they had available for the flags. They offered to use my mom's brother's flag in the military parades and ceremonies they perform throughout the year at the cemetery. They offered to put my dad's flag and case in their visitor's center, displayed with others who had served our country. We thought these options were perfect ways to honor our relatives and their service.

When all the dots connected, the things that made little sense at first now made perfect sense. It was the ideal place for my dad's flag. It was near where I lived, and if I wanted, I could go there and see it. At that moment, I was thankful and understood why I bought the better-quality display case, even though at the time I fussed at myself for buying something I couldn't even display.

Your Thoughts About Them Change

My parents are different people to me now than when they were alive. I loved them, but I didn't always like them. There had been a lot of neglect throughout my childhood. Then a lot more negligence, as adults, on both sides of the relationship. Over the years, there were times I chose not to see or talk to either of them. But those irritating things, or unpleasant events, the things they said or did, all have disappeared one by one since they died.

Now, I find it almost impossible to mention anything adverse. I don't like others saying harsh things about them, either. I don't know if this change is just a normal part of the grieving process. Perhaps it is. This is also why you won't find many details about unpleasant events or any hateful comments about my parents in this book.

I'm amazed how, over time, my feelings about my parents have softened. Perhaps grieving makes that happen. If so, I'm glad it does. It'll allow you to let go of things. You'll finally give them the benefit of the doubt. You may realize that you didn't or couldn't allow yourself to experience the full capacity of the situation, the people involved, and your feelings about it at the time when it happened. Although a lot of the pain has gone, I still have a few things that come up or something that I remember from time to time. Mostly I miss them, both of them. And sometimes I miss one more than the other. This doesn't seem to ever go away, and honestly, I don't think I want it to go away completely.

I honor them in better ways now. Missing them is a form of that. They were the most important people in my life, and they had the most significant effect on me; who I am, and how I relate to things. The little things I do with my hands or how I talk, these physical or personality traits that I mimic, are dear to me now. But I remember times when those things thoroughly irritated and annoyed me. I've always seen both of them in my face when I peer into a mirror. People will say I resemble one or the other, but I see them both. I feel the different effects each had on who I've become and who I'll still grow to become.

My mom had a shift in her thinking after she went with me on that 2,000-mile journey to my dad's home to take care of him. Right away, I had to make several tough decisions, and she saw me as an adult for the first time in my life. Had she seen herself reflected in me? I learned a lot of that resilience and tenacity from her in my younger years. She'd just never seen it in me.

When we got there, she saw his home's condition and the room full of boxes and piles of papers. She listened to me on the phone night after night telling her aboutsifting through the dusty, moldy things in his home. During that time, she decided she would start going through her belongings and try to make it easier for me when the time came. Thank you, mom!

Before she died, she'd gone through quite a lot and got rid of items that no longer served her. I was thankful we had adult conversations concerning these things. She told me it impressed her when I went to take care of my dad, even though it meant giving up everything. Because of that experience, she wanted to make it easier for me when she died. But neither of us thought she would die so soon.

CHAPTER 17
HIS THINGS, HER THINGS, YOUR THINGS

A few years before my parents died, I decided to lighten my load during one of my moves. One of the things I parted with was a large box with all the photos I had accumulated throughout my life. There were photos from my teenage years, ones from my twenties, and more from my thirties and forties when I had taken up photography as a hobby.

I knew they would cause a mixed-bag of emotions if I browsed through them. I'd catch myself saying things like, "Oh, I should keep this one and that one, too." Next thing you know, I've kept 75% of the photos and spent two-hours walking down memory lane. But on that day, I decided I didn't need those photos any longer. So, without even peering into the box, I tossed it in the trash bin. And no, I didn't go back for it later. My focus that day was on moving several thousand miles away, so I don't think I gave it another thought then or later.

When I was 17 years old, I received a small photo album. I keep it inside its original box. It has a beautiful Japanese-inspired illustration of a heron and grasses growing by a stream on a black lacquered front cover with a blank, matching black back cover. Inside are photos of close friends, former boyfriends, a few pictures of my parents from earlier years, some of my favorite aunts and uncles, and a few of my cousins. These may be the only photos I ever had of or the only ones I wanted to keep of them. I wouldn't just toss these in a trash bin and walk away.

When my dad died, I became the owner of his photo albums. He had all my baby pictures, lots of them, photos I had never seen and photographs from my school years. There were old photos of his parents and siblings and pictures of him and his first wife. Images of other people whom I presume were his aunts and uncles. A few had familiar names, but I didn't recall ever meeting any of them. I'm not sure if they were still alive when I was born or not.

I took these photos out of their old crusty photo albums and tossed the albums. There was a picture of a naked girl; no idea who, toss. There were photos from my wedding. Those damn wedding photos. I had thrown the originals off a bridge after my divorce. I had tossed them all, except for the one, my favorite "one." Okay, now I have a box of pictures again.

Fast forward two years, my mom has died, and I'm going through her things and delegating their future. Oh, lovely, another box of photos. This time the photographs are of her family. Again, I heard their names a few times, but I don't recall their faces or ever meeting them. I found several interesting ones, followed by "Hey, wait a minute! I'm not proficient with math, but this doesn't up to the story I overheard about these people." Hmm, decisions . . . "Nope, don't want to know!" Choosing ignorance can be bliss. "Oh geez, no, not those damn wedding photos, again! Yep, definitely trash. No, I don't need to look through them again." Toss. I added her photos to the box of the ones from my dad. "Oh, wonderful, now I have a larger box of photos!"

I did decide I thought it was worth my time to scan them and create a digital photo library. I don't get those nostalgic feelings when I look at photos on the computer. Those feelings that can happen when you flip through pages or stacks of Kodaks and Polaroids. But yes, there they are, those damn wedding photos again. I managed to camouflage the digital versions on my computer with the hundreds of other folders full of images.

No One Would Know Them

There I was spending hours and hours scanning and saving photos onto my computer. During the second or third batch of hours, I started questioning why I was doing all this scanning and saving. Who was I saving them for? Who would acknowledge that it was me in those baby pictures? They wouldn't discern the two-year-old boy standing on the man's knee was my dad with his father. No one would recognize my mom and her siblings sporting their curlicue curls and slicked-back hair in that old photo from the 1940's. Nor the image of my grandparents in their 1930's garb. The picture of my parents on their wedding day wouldn't be valuable to anyone. No one could care one way or another about those damn wedding photos of mine. It's just another one of those instances that comes at you from left field. Something that, until it does, may not have even crossed your mind.

I finished scanning them a few months ago, but I haven't tossed the box of photos yet. It will need to be one of those "don't open the box!" moments, just throw it in and walk away. A few days ago, I was online and saw an online store selling old pictures. Was there a market for these old photos? Were people buying photographs of people they didn't know? There appeared to be a use for the pictures other than rubbish. This could be a potential solution for the photos other than tossing them. The seller had used generic captions such as, "People in the late 1950's in wedding attire cutting their wedding cake." Price $6.

Do you have old pictures of your family that you are not sure what to do with them? Did you inherit photos from your parents? How were photographs displayed in your home? Were there photo albums on the bookshelves or portraits displayed in frames on the walls? Did you have any of those photos taken at a department store or photography studio where everyone has matching outfits? What are you planning to do with your photos? If you tossed them, get them back if you can -- you could make a few bucks here!

Decide if you feel comfortable selling pictures of your family. You will be selling them to people whom you do not know who are buying photographs of people who are strangers to them. You also don't know what they plan to do with the photos, either. Strange? Yes? No? This will be a personal decision for you.

To Hear Their Voice Again

Nowadays, we can keep lots of voicemails. We can preserve memories in ways that were not available until a few years ago. Right after your parent died, when your grief was full-blown, you may forget about the voicemails and texts on your phone. You might forget that your phone will drop an older voicemail to make room for a new one.

And one day, you remember and scroll through them. You realize you lost the ones your dad left you when he was in the hospital. "Oh, wait, here's one…" Tap, listen, frown. Oh geez, the only message from him I still had, was from the night he called from the hospital talking about all kinds of crazy stuff. He told me to call the Fire Department in the city 2,000 miles away where he had worked and ask them to get there because he was being kept against his will. Unfortunately, I lost any other voicemail messages from my dad to keep as a remembrance.

I found out later from the doctors that when people in their 70's and 80's get UTIs, this crazy behavior is a common symptom. It was one of the strangest things I learned about aging. Not sure why it affects older people this way. It's an odd thing to see your parent hallucinating, acting crazy, and really believing all the nonsense they're spouting.

This same infection preempted the ambulance ride, which led to my mom's hospital stay after the neighbor called me and said my mom was talking crazy and not acting like herself.

When the EMTs got there, they checked her vitals and then called me. She had a fever and several other symptoms, and they said she should go to the hospital, and she agreed to have them take her.

After my mom died, I had a comparable situation with the voicemail messages she had left me. Again, I remembered a little too late about them getting deleted. There was only one still on my phone, and it was from the day before she died. She said, she just wanted to go home and didn't understand why she didn't feel any better. She sounded so sad. It wasn't a message I wanted to keep, even if it was her voice.

Finding Treasures

I still check my parent's email accounts periodically, and several months after my mom died, I was checking her account. As you unsubscribe them from newsletters and email lists, the number of emails you receive for them will decrease. I also recommend you monitor their credit reports for at least two years.

My mom had used her computer for things like email, finding stuff on the internet, doing some shopping, and saving photos from her camera with ease. She even learned how to make spreadsheets and use banking applications. After I reconnected with her when my dad got sick, I introduced her to a smartphone and taught her how to send text messages. I also showed her how to take photos and attach and send them in a text message. Sometimes when she was trying to do something, she would get things mixed up, but it would work anyhow. If you asked how she did it, she couldn't tell you for sure.

One day, I was going through my old emails, and I found one from my mom with an audio attachment. Somehow, she had recorded a voicemail and then emailed it to me using her phone. This wasn't something I had shown her how to do. In fact, I had discouraged her from using her cellphone for email because it was too hard to read and manage them on the small screen. Her message said there was an issue with her home phone and internet. I was out of town that day, and she wanted me to know what was happening so that I wouldn't worry if I couldn't reach her. After my dad died, she didn't want me worrying about too many things tried not to bother me with the small stuff. The message ended with those three heartfelt words, "I love you." Bonus!

This message was such a treasure. You'll find your strongest remembrances of them are those which affect your senses. When you hear a person's voice, they need not tell you who they are. You already recognize it's them. This has been the best gift I received after my mom died. Treasures like this can help the only-only (O^2) during their grieving process. I think it can also be beneficial even for those who aren't only-children.

CHAPTER 18
WHERE DO I FIT?

Where do I fit? I thought some change in my life would initiate "a group for that," and it would be perfect for me. When I was growing up, everyone I knew had a brother(s) and/or sister(s). None of my friends or other relatives were only-children.

I always thought I was different, but I didn't always correlate it with being an only-child. If I mentioned this to someone, they thought I meant I was "special" because I was an only-child. It's not how I meant it. I didn't believe I was "special." I thought I was an "oddball."

When I joined a church in my late 20's, there was a group for singles, but they were all younger than I was. Everyone at church, at work, and my neighbors were all married, had kids, or both. I didn't fit into any of those groups. I didn't have any comments or funny stories with children to help create an interesting conversation. Without siblings, I have no nieces or nephews either. I could tell them a tale about my cat or the neighbor's dog, but, well, you see my point.

I got married in my early 30's and thought, now I'll be part of a group. Nope, again, I didn't fit in with them, either. The younger married people were dealing with struggles that weren't the same struggles I was experiencing. As I got into my late 30's and early 40's and still didn't have children, I didn't fit anywhere. The married people were now in their 40's, separated or divorced, and many had grandchildren!

The most significant component in these groups was most people had siblings, and this one shift made us different. I noticed their friendships even differed from mine. Their friends were just friends, not family.

Would I Say That About You?

Everyone has 20/20 vision when confronted by their past actions and their responses to your actions. If you have spent most of your life making sure everyone else was okay, take this time now to make sure *you're* okay. Don't buy into the stereotypical thinking that you are selfish. You are not. But believing these things may have affected many of your decisions.

People don't label other family members in these derogatory ways. You don't meet someone with a sibling and say to them, "Wow, I bet you're a spoiled brat!" Meaning in a rotten way, something you throw away! The comment implies you have an automatic prerequisite entitling your parents to spoil you. Do you meet an uncle and inquire, "Are you a reclusive weirdo?" Because everyone concludes that uncles resemble those types, right? Would you say to a divorced person, "I heard divorcees are self-centered and socially awkward, but you seem normal." How rude would that be?

It can mess you up when you're young because the last thing you want to be is this awful thing that they're "betting" or "heard" you are. It's not like you made a choice to be an only-child. When you become old enough to realize what they're implying, you do everything in your power to be the exact opposite of those things. How can people assume what type of person we are just because we're an only-child? Today, the law protects people from stereotypes or people who single them out as different — and no laws protect only-children from these people.

What Do You Say About You?

If those stereotypes still play in your head, you need to give it another melody to listen to and change the lyrics. It's time to take back your identity and throw the labels in the garbage. Others within our minority share your unique view of the world as an only-child. Don't be ashamed of your advantages. To not use these gifts is disrespectful to yourself and others. If you had a rotten childhood and your family sucked, you may not think being an only-child has given you any benefits. First, I'm sorry that was your experience. But it has made you who you are, and it's your choice now as an adult only-child to change it to your gain.

The picture may not be clear until you get much older and give yourself the freedom to be you. I would bet that you didn't notice many things until you no longer had on the parent blinders. But even with the chaos, unpleasantness, and anger of your childhood, you're extraordinary. You can make an impact, find where you fit, and help others like yourself. Only you keep you stuck, and I know this from experience.

Thank you for the Compliment

Being around adults is easy for me, and I'm even more comfortable around those older than I. That ability comes from spending so much more time with adults when I was a child. Two of my closest friends are 15 years older than I am. Like me as a child, you may have spent more time with adults than with children your own age.

Are you more comfortable with yourself or being by yourself? Do you think you know yourself better than others know themselves? Many people aren't friends with themselves. They're not okay with being alone for short periods; more extended periods are out of the question, and others can't be by themselves at all. For most only-children, being alone recharges us. Our quietness allows us to listen to the stillness. It's something that others experience so seldom, it can scare them.

What do you think of the stereotypical only-child comments? Do they make you question yourself and who you are? I suggest you take those stereotypical comments as compliments. People spend lots of time and money to gain the strength we come by naturally. You need to change the voice inside you, uttering that being an only-child is a dreadful thing. We may lack other social skills, and if we never gain them, it doesn't mean we're broken; we're just different.

Not What I Planned

I started making adult decisions early in life. I was independent and wasn't comfortable asking for help. Others didn't offer me support because I gave people the impression that I had it together and didn't need help. That was usually not even close to the truth, but I had learned I had to buck up, get over myself, dust my butt off, and keep going. Is your life what you planned? Is the life you created the one you wanted?

I didn't choose all of the realities in my life, it's just how my life turned out, and I try to make the best of it. Most parents envision a picture of their child having their grandchildren and then those grandchildren having their great-grandchildren. But not everyone's life is the norm, nor do they want it that way. Now that I'm older, I'm thankful I don't have children (and no, it doesn't make me selfish).

There may be disagreement over this, but I wonder about the parent who has siblings that believes their child is better off without siblings. Did they have an experience that makes them think there is some benefit negated by having a sibling? That belief doesn't guarantee their child will be better without them. They also don't have any experience of being an only-child to back up their opinion. Unless they were the firstborn and had at least five, closer to seven years, before they had a sibling, then they were never an only-child. A second- or later-born child never experiences being an only-child because they'll always have the firstborn as a sibling.

It would be analogous to tell someone they shouldn't be a parent or say to them they're better off not having children. Yes, I had parents and know other parents, but I've never been a parent. I have nothing to use as a reference. My experience of not having children doesn't mean they'll realize the same results, and I have nothing to back up the comment.

The challenges of the adult only-child are distinctive in their effects compared to an adult with siblings, as the only-child becomes an adult (not just acts like one). These challenges increase their conclusiveness later in life, for example, when their parent(s) die. This life event can devastate the adult only-child who finds themselves an only-only (O^2) with no support.

CHAPTER 19
A COMMON REFLECTION

Have you ever examined the interaction between people who meet for the first time? People tend to gravitate toward other people with common traits and spend time with people who have similar interests. You can connect with these people, and they generate growth in your life. They confirm the way you process things.

One of the most common connections is children. It doesn't matter whether it's a single parent or a couple. Their children are a part of their reflection. There are conditions of, or experiences specific to, being a parent, and they will recognize those reflections in another parent. It's the same for those with siblings. The likeness exists between them, regardless of whether they have a good relationship with the siblings. Other similarities and commonalities will create more angles within the reflections.

Another only-child will "get" why you decide the things you do. They won't think anything is wrong with you or the way you process your life. In fact, your validation may give them the courage to get through their tough times too. You may find solace in your only-ness but also wish to find others who reflect you. This can be a life-changer for all of us.

As an only-child, your only-ness will reflect in your connection with another only-child. If your parents have died, this will appear, too. If you don't have children, this will add another facet. It's another aspect within the reflection. It doesn't matter whether it was your choice or a choice made by nature. Other elements include having no significant other or extended family. These add angles to the pieces of your reflection. This person reflects an adult only-child + orphan + childless + lives alone + no extended family = an only-only (O^2).

Not Identical, but Identifiable

I get frustrated when I read comments that follow online articles written about only-children. The words turn into debates about who had it better or worse, those with or those without siblings. It's not a competition, and the answer is, we all did. Life has pleasant aspects and unpleasant aspects. The article loses any valuable points that the author may have made.

What's important is finding the support you need and the answers you're looking for when you need them. It seemed ironic that the death of my parents, which left me more alone than I had been in my entire life, would lead me to the place where I fit -- to people who, when they said they were sorry for my loss, would appreciate the enormity of what that meant to me.

As only-children, we're not identical, but our similar traits make us identifiable. As a collective group, we can gain strength from these similarities and let go of any shame around the stereotypical labels. Even though I had a deep bond with my parents, they both had siblings. There was no realistic way they could relate to me as an only-child. Do you find the people who understand and can easily connect to you are other only-children? This support and sense of belonging comes from those with the same reflection.

I Don't Have Those

Does it seem that everyone you know has a child, a grandchild, a great-grandchild, a niece or nephew, an in-law, or a significant other? More importantly, you realize that they're not alone. They didn't spend the last four years moving back and forth across the country, taking care of their parent(s) and the lives they left behind. These responsibilities left you plagued with a lot of life issues and the accompanying emotions. Intimate relationships or keeping friendships is not feasible when you move thousands of miles away every six months.

It hasn't been two weeks for most people since they spoke to someone they thought cared about them (and the cashier at the store doesn't count). They're not grappling with the loss of the business they had just started building, losing capital they invested, loss of income, and loss of self-worth. They're not reeling from the loss of a pet they had to leave behind, besides the loss of the two most influential people in their life. I tried to find someone, anyone, that I could talk with about these things. What I found is most people can't fathom that level of being alone.

I longed my entire life for a place where I fit. A place people accepted my solo style of thinking and doing things. These people get why it's not so easy for me to go out and make a lot of new friends. They understand why it matters if people have children or siblings. It hadn't occurred to me that I had people, and I could be the one to bring them together. Like me, other people were wondering and asking the same questions and still searching for the answers.

Nothing Wrong with Who You Are

The advice in this book is here to help make things easier for you. To receive help from someone who's not concerned with why you're the way you are because of your parents or because you're an only-child. Examine the picture of your family and be aware of how it looks to you. I wasn't aware until later that even after they divorced many years ago, the image was always the three of us. Although now I only see me.

During this time, when your parents are no longer affecting your life, you may feel you're losing yourself, too. Use the information found in this book to help you when you're struggling to find your importance. Your worth is when you realize the difference you can make when connecting with another adult only-child.

CHAPTER 20
YOUR UNIQUE PLACE

You're in a unique position as the only-child and heir. This is the best part of this situation, and it can be even better. You'll avoid spending valuable time and energy second-guessing your decisions if your parent(s) completed these important documents and essential tasks:

- Power of Attorney
- Health Care Directives
  - including a DNR
- Last will and testament and/or created a trust
- Convert properties into joint ownership
- Gather important papers in one place
  - Property titles and deeds
  - Birth certificates
  - Military records
  - Divorce and/or marriage records
  - Property and life insurance records
  - Bank and other financial records
- Plans for their pets
- Discuss any collections they own

- Plans for their burial or cremation
  - Preferred funeral home
  - Burial plots and headstones
  - Choose where to spread their ashes

You'll have to make many difficult decisions about their care if they don't complete these tasks and become incapacitated. If they've died, you must do a quick study of the probate system. Be ready to pay fees, spend time at the courthouse to file paperwork, or find and pay for an excellent lawyer. It will entail figuring out things as you go, a lot of things! It will overwhelm you if you are totally alone.

By having those adult conversations with your parent(s) before they die, it'll help you now and later. If you don't have them, you can get through it. It'll just be more demanding. Your growth and experiences can help someone else. Encourage others not to wait. Don't think there will be time later. Today is the perfect day to start the discussions and put those plans together.

Losing and Finding Yourself

You may lose yourself when you're dealing with the loss of your parent(s). This is the most challenging part of this life event. It can pick up your entire world and turn it over like an hourglass as you watch the sand slide from one side to the other. How do you respond to that? Everyone has this reserve of strength that we dim or turn off like a light. An only-only (O^2) has an even larger reserve, which comes from the unique characteristics of who we are.

An only-only (O^2) interprets the distinction between solitude and loneliness. Most of us can do isolation with a smile. Use your quiet determination to help others. Another only-child grants you the validation you need when they say they know how you feel or what you mean, because they do! Out of the only-child types, the only-only (O^2) is unique in their ability to change the surrounding environment. Just being aware of other only's is enough to strengthen us and to give us courage.

To realize someone out there "gets" us. Our people are waiting for an invitation to come together. Let's support each other and cheer each other on as we reach goals and milestones. Get the word out to the other adult only-children and spread this hope to those in this challenging position.

Who Can I Help?

I want to help that person not feel as lonely as I did. To be the person who appreciates and is familiar with the adult only-child's challenges in navigating this part of your life. To be a support and a calmness in your storm. I'll tell you it's okay for you to do what's right for you, that you're not selfish, and you're a responsible adult. There will be setbacks, but you'll get through this. You think no one empathizes and that something is wrong with you. In fact, nothing is wrong with you.

That's precisely where I found myself. I thought no one understood me. Although only a few people were there, I kept looking for the person who could reflect my only-ness. There were so many decisions to make, so much I had to figure out. Guidance from another adult only-child would've been helpful. Someone who understood the importance of hearing someone say that I was doing the right things even if I did it wrong.

When you're in that space, I am someone who understands. Another only-child can empathize with you after your parent has died, and it can be beneficial when other only's validate you. Yes, other people's parents die, but it's different for an only-child, and it's okay that it's different. I got overjoyed and then scared when I realized this was my journey. My life had been preparing me for this. I became aware of how scared the adult only-child was in their body and mind, as they stood there, all alone. It was an enormous, dry, scorching desert with no trees, no water, no life-giving support, as if there were no air.

The adult only-child wants more than anything to connect to someone who understands them. Even if it's just one other person. Reach out to me, and I can be the calm voice and hand that reaches out and says, "I'm here." Together we can research those things you need to figure out. I want to make it easier for you to get through this sorrow and to let you know you're not alone; you're not the only-only (O^2).

Who qualifies as an only-only (O^2)?

If you can answer yes to these four key points, you're an only-only (O^2) and have found your people!

- **No siblings.**
  - This includes step-siblings, half-siblings, and any other combinations of the sort.
- **No children.**
  - You have children if you love the children of your significant other as your own.
- **No parents.**
  - Both parents have died, including adopted or foster parents. You have a parent if your biological parent(s) is alive, and you have a relationship with them, regardless of whether they raised you.
- **No significant other.**
  - Includes those living in the same dwelling with you, such as friends or roommates.

If your parent has died recently, you need the support and guidance of another only-only (O^2) now more than ever. Another only-only (O^2) is either where you are now or has been where you are and can help you in ways no one else can.

Support for the Only-Only (O^2)

What support would you like to see available in the only-only (O^2) community? Is there a particular need we could focus on that affects us? What types of vulnerabilities are you dealing with because of the losses in your life? Contact me at joy@onlysquared.com with ideas, suggestions, and comments.

• • •

DEFINITIONS AND INFORMATION

Advance Directive Forms

These forms are state-specific and can differ from state to state depending on the laws governing someone's death. Check your state government website. Usually, these forms are available to print out at no charge.

Advance Care Planning

National Hospice and Palliative Care Organization (NHPCO)
https://www.nhpco.org/patients-and-caregivers/

Checklists to Use after Someone Dies

https://www.aarp.org/home-family/friends-family/info-2020/
when-loved-one-dies-checklist.html

https://www.consumerreports.org/family/what-to-do-when-
a-loved-one-dies/

Estate Sales

An estate sale or estate liquidation is a sale or auction to dispose
of a substantial portion of the materials owned by a recently
deceased person or someone who must dispose of their personal
property to facilitate a move.

For more information: NESA – National Estate Sales
Association at https://nesa-usa.com

Last Will and Testament

A Last Will and Testament is a legal document allowing you
to control your estate's distribution after your death. You can
use it to appoint a guardian for your minor children. You can
also set aside funds and instructions for the care of your pets.

For more information: https://en.wikipedia.org/wiki/
Will_and_testament

Notary Public in the United States

This is an official of integrity appointed by state government —
typically by the secretary of state — to serve the public as an
impartial witness in performing various official fraud-deterrent
acts related to the signing of important documents. These official acts are notarizations or notarial acts.

For more information: https://www.nationalnotary.org/
knowledge-center/about-notaries

Trusts

A trust is a fiduciary arrangement that allows a third party, or trustee, to hold assets on behalf of a beneficiary or beneficiaries. You can arrange a trust in many ways and specify precisely how and when the assets pass to the beneficiaries.

For more information: https://en.wikipedia.org/wiki/Trust_law

• • •

Notes

Notes

Notes

Notes

Notes

Made in the USA
Coppell, TX
19 December 2021